THE
VERMONT
FARM TO TABLE
COOKBOOK

OVER 50 FRESH & LOCAL RECIPES FOR EVERY SEASON

Nora Ricc & Jenna Rice

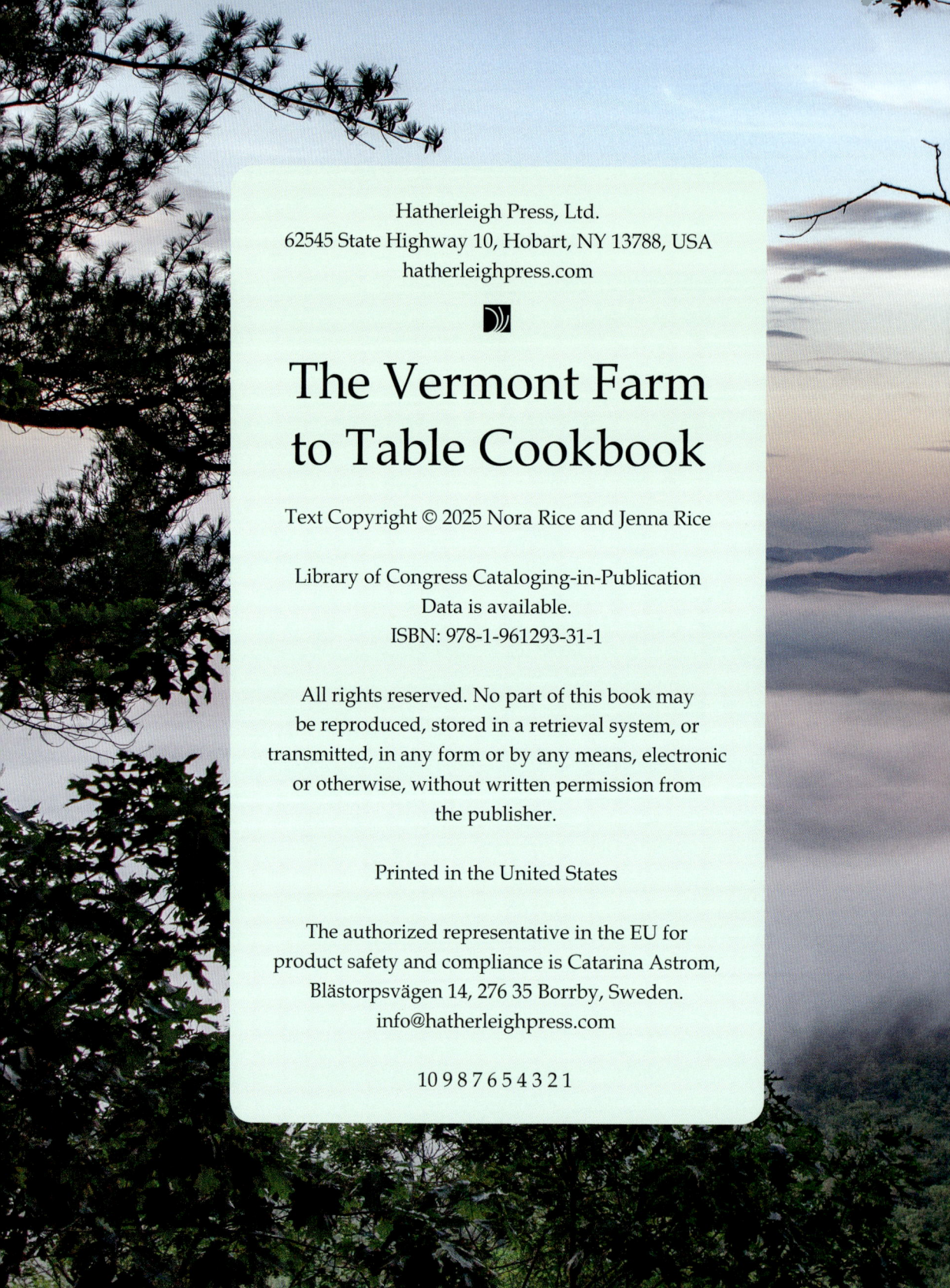

Hatherleigh Press, Ltd.
62545 State Highway 10, Hobart, NY 13788, USA
hatherleighpress.com

The Vermont Farm to Table Cookbook

Library of Congress Cataloging-in-Publication
Data is available.
ISBN: 978-1-961293-31-1

Printed in the United States

The authorized representative in the EU for
product safety and compliance is Catarina Astrom,
Blästorpsvägen 14, 276 35 Borrby, Sweden.
info@hatherleighpress.com

10 9 8 7 6 5 4 3 2 1

To our parents Beth and Phil,
for always supporting us in
creating our own paths in life

Contents

Preface

Driving north through the eastern part of Vermont, with the Green Mountains to your left and the Connecticut River below to your right, you are surrounded by farms. The deep soil of the river valley land makes a good place to put down roots — for plants and people alike.

I-91 runs alongside the river, but when you get off of the highway and wind your way along back roads, that's where you really start to see the heart and soul of Vermont. Centuries old barns, some falling to ruin, and others kept alive by the hard-working hands of one or two devoted people. Stone walls piled along the sides of roads, each stone resting where it was placed by unknown hands, at an unknown date a long time ago. It is on one of these hills, near one of the still surviving barns surrounded by stone walls, where we spent our childhood.

The town of Hartland is not a particularly notable one, lacking the historic mansions that draw crowds of visitors to nearby Woodstock. Its modest town center is home to just a general store, post office, and small diner, all arranged around a central parking lot, and next to an odd 5½ way intersection whose layout has been the subject of disagreement for decades.

When we were young, we learned to ride our bikes along our dirt road and spent our summers splashing in the pond on the far side of our family's land. When we were old enough, we would ride our bikes to the general store in town, pool our cash, and gorge ourselves on every kind of candy and junk food we could find.

Growing up on a Vermont farm, I guess you could say that as children we took good food for granted. It was not "farm to table" food, or local organic superfoods, it was just food. As young adults, we began lives of our own, and in the typical way, survived on primarily cold pizza and ramen. It was not until several years later that we each in our own way reconnected with the land, with Vermont, and with local food systems.

Nora attended culinary school in England, and then moved back to the States, working in restaurants in Seattle, then Montana. She then returned to Europe, this time living and cooking in Italy, then Ireland, and then New Zealand, learning about the local food systems of each place. I stayed in Vermont, in the same river valley where we grew up, and after a few different jobs, and a few different apartments, I settled on a six-acre homestead with the man who would become my husband, and started my business as a photographer and designer, all while constantly expanding my gardens and acquiring new farm animals on the side.

It was when Nora returned from living abroad in New Zealand that the idea for Local Pantry was born. Out of a shared love for food, farming, and creativity, came the idea to create a book of recipes from the local land. Good, healthy food is so abundant right here in Vermont, and seeing a constant stream of trendy recipes calling for superfoods grown thousands of miles away shines a light on the thing that is missing; healthy, real food that I can watch turn from a seed to a plant to a meal. Food that I can see not only nourishing myself and my family, but also my neighbors, local farms, the local economy, and the earth. There is more than one way to define healthy, but it goes beyond the way that food affects one's body. You can't ignore the health of the person who harvested the food for low wages, the pollution burdening our earth and our bodies caused by shipping that food around the world, and the plastic waste left over when all is said and done.

In a way it has been done before, and the idea of farm to table recipes is nothing new, but *The Vermont Farm to Table Cookbook* brings the local ingredients theme to a new level, using exclusively Vermont-grown ingredients, with only the tiny exception for things like salt and cooking oil. We hope that you will find in this book the same thing that we find here in Vermont—a sense of place, a sense of connection, and of course, delicious food!

—Jenna

Welcome to Vermont

The contrasting seasons of Vermont combined with the gently mountainous landscape offer a sense of place so distinct that only an hour's long drive will take you away to an entirely different world. Our mountains do not tower along the skyline, but instead roll more gently along the horizon, still framing the landscape in gentle peaks. The sky is small here, small and comforting. Rarely can you see the whole horizon for the trees standing in your way. But when you do find yourself on top of one of these gentle mountains, when you really can see everything, it will take your breath away.

Compared to other places, people will tell you Vermont is not the easiest place to grow food. Perhaps this is true—those same mountains that stand along the horizon have all around them left stones throughout the soil. The growing season is not long here, but it is just long enough. You can't grow everything, but you can grow everything you need.

Every April, spring brings with it edible plants hidden and tucked away in the shadows of hillsides and on the banks of rivers and streams. After a long winter, the people and wild animals alike long for new beginnings, and for fresh foods! And just in time, spring greens pop up in gardens all across the land, and if you know where to look, hidden fields of wild leeks and fiddlehead ferns are bountiful.

Summer is fleeting, and that makes it all the more beautiful. Berries bursting forth on every bush, ripe tomatoes drooping on the vine, and sweet corn, if only you can beat the raccoons to it! Summer days are long, but the season itself is short, giving it a nostalgic feel, frozen in time.

Fall may be the most iconic season for Vermont and all of New England, and visitors flock here to see the trees turn color. But fall brings another kind of excitement too— harvest season! The time when every food is ready for the picking, bursting with flavor and vibrant color. And the options for meals from the land seem limitless.

Winter brings with it a deep calm. A slowing down of the mind, of the routines, and of time itself. Winter is a time for reflection, for rest, and for comfort food. A time for slowly enjoying the bounty of the past months, with root cellars and pantries stocked with the staples: potatoes, dry beans and corn, carrots, and cabbage, and freezers full of frozen veggies and meat.

This book will offer you new perspectives on cooking from the local land, on growing your own food, and on making that food into meals without relying on outside ingredients. Every ingredient listed on these pages can be grown in your own garden or found at a farmstand just down the road. Just like the land, food is unique to a place, and unique to a moment in time, tied to the changing of the seasons. The best food you will ever taste won't be shipped halfway around the world; it will be harvested right where you live. Maybe it is the freshness that brings out the superior flavors, or maybe the knowledge and understanding that is mixed throughout the meal adds that additional flavor, that "taste of place."

Growing
Pantry Staples

Many home gardeners tend to focus on greens, tomatoes, zucchini, and all of those summer crops. And for good reason—a fresh tomato is not even similar to the sad, pale, barely-red tomatoes that you might find in a supermarket. But storage crops and staples are often overlooked, and many of these crops can grow easily here in Vermont and offer nutritious food and superior flavors year-round. Dry beans, flour corn, potatoes, cabbage, and winter squash are among those often overlooked staples. Many of these staples are surprisingly easy to cultivate, and can yield bountiful harvests, enough to last through the winter.

Flour Corn

Similar to dry beans, if you have ever grown sweet corn, then you more or less already know how to grow flour corn. If you have ever grown decorative "Indian corn" then you have actually already grown flour corn, as these beautiful ears can not only be used for decoration but can also be ground into cornmeal or polenta.

When growing corn of any variety, it is important to have a patch at least four rows wide. Corn is wind pollinated and having a larger patch gives you a better chance of harvesting nice full ears. However, you can always help your corn out by shaking a few of the tassels near the young ears, helping to ensure successful pollination.

Wait for the husks of your corn to dry before harvesting the ears. After harvest, unwrap the ears and place them on a wire rack or screen to ensure good airflow while they dry. Once the corn is fully dry, twist the kernels off of the ears and store them in airtight containers. Wait to grind your cornmeal until you are ready to use it to ensure maximum freshness. Small hand crank mills are fairly inexpensive and can be used to grind your corn at home. I keep most of my corn in the pantry in kernel form but keep a quart jar of ground cornmeal in the kitchen cabinet, at the ready.

Dry Beans

Dry beans are one of my favorite storage crops to grow, simply because they are so easy to store. Once dried, beans can be kept for a year or longer in airtight containers. No refrigeration is necessary, and the flavor and textures of different heirloom beans are nuanced and delicious. If you are already growing green beans, then you know just about everything that you need to know. Plant the seeds after the danger of frost has passed, about four inches apart and one inch deep. Unlike green beans, you won't be harvesting until a bit later in the season, but very little maintenance is required, other than an occasional weeding. Even that is kept to a minimum as the leafy bush beans shade out most weeds. When the pods begin to turn brown, pick them and shell the beans into baskets. Allow them to air dry for several weeks, then store the beans in airtight containers.

Some of my favorite fall evenings have been spent sitting on the porch with a few friends, chatting away and shelling beans. You look down after a good conversation to find that the beans are all shelled, and you didn't even notice.

And one more bonus, there are dozens of varieties of gorgeous heirloom beans, almost too pretty to eat, and you can easily keep your own seed. Since beans are self-pollinated you needn't worry about cross pollination, and you can set aside a few of your beans to plant in the spring!

Potatoes

There is something really fun about growing potatoes—almost like magic. You bury one tuber in the spring and when you return to dig it up in the fall, that one tuber has multiplied into a dozen!

You might think that a potato is a potato and there can't be much difference between the homegrown variety and the ones you find in a supermarket, but you couldn't be more wrong.

Dozens of potato varieties are available to the home gardener, each boasting of different desirable traits. From the bright purple Magic Molly potatoes, which are purple through to the center, to the smooth and creamy German Butterball, a small golden potato with the creamiest texture I have ever tasted. A homegrown potato has a firm consistency, complex flavor, and beautiful smooth skin, unlike your average supermarket spud. Potatoes can be a fantastic staple in your diet, especially throughout the winter and early spring, and they are absolutely delicious in recipes like our Smashed Yukon Gem Potatoes (p. 139) and Potato and Wild Leek Gratin (p. 47).

Cabbage

Cabbage is not exactly a flashy vegetable, but it is highly underrated. As one of the few green veggies that can easily be stored fresh, cabbage holds an important place in a winter pantry. Cabbage is also quite easy to grow even in a cold northern climate, as the plants are not particularly sensitive to the cold temperatures. I leave my cabbages in the field until mid-October, before harvesting and storing them in my root cellar, packed in crates filled with damp wood shavings to keep the cabbages from drying out. Different varieties of cabbage offer different advantages, such as sweet flavor, or interesting color. I grow Storage No. 4, which, as the name implies, is known for its long shelf life—this is essential as I need my cabbages to remain fresh all the way through the winter. Cabbage plants do need to be started in pots indoors, but they are hardy and would be the perfect plant to practice on if you are new to seed starting.

Winter Squash

If you have grown zucchini or summer squash, then you are capable of growing winter squash for storage. Similar to summer squash, you will need to start your plants indoors in early May and allow the plants to grow for several weeks before transplanting them to the garden around Memorial Day. Alternatively, you can find pre-started plants of some more common winter squash varieties, such as acorn and butternut, at your local farm store. But if you want to branch out and explore the true diversity of flavors in the winter squash world, then you will want to start your own plants from seed. Winter squash plants grow fast and will quickly shade out weeds, so they will be quite low maintenance for most of the growing season. But be warned, they will take up a lot of space, so make sure you don't plant them too close to your other plants. Leave your squash to grow all summer, waiting to harvest until you see frost coming in the weather forecast. Once you harvest, store your squash in a dry space, ideally with the temperature around 50 degrees. Depending on the variety you have chosen, you may want to wait a month or two to enjoy your squash, allowing them to "cure" and develop more flavor. Varieties like Delicata and Acorn can be eaten right away, but Butternut and Kabocha are best after some time has passed.

Responsible Foraging

Vermont is abundant with wild edible plants and mushrooms and knowing how to forage safely and responsibly is a huge topic that could fill an entire other book (in fact, there are many great books available on this topic).

Wild leeks, also known as ramps, and fiddlehead ferns are the two wild edible plants that are featured in Local Pantry. Both of these plants thrive in Vermont, and with a little bit of practice you will be able to spot them easily.

It is important when foraging for any wild plant to take only what you need and leave behind much more than you take so that the plants can go on to reproduce and the population can continue to thrive. With ramps in particular, it is best to take only one leaf per plant, allowing the rest of the plant to survive. Ramps take several years to become mature enough to reproduce, so I only dig bulbs (thus killing the plant) from a large patch where I know that I am the only one picking and can be sure that I am only taking a handful out of the thousands of bulbs. Otherwise, I stick to picking only one leaf here and there.

A similar principle can be applied to fiddlehead ferns. Each plant will produce around ten fiddleheads, which if not picked will fan out and become ferns later in the season. When picking fiddleheads, only take a couple out of the ten or so that the plant still produces, leaving a majority to go on and support the plant throughout the season.

Ramps and fiddleheads are both abundant, and it is in our hands to take good care of these amazing plants, helping them to thrive enough that there are plenty for us to enjoy without harming the patch!

Shopping for Local Ingredients

One of the great things about Vermont is the accessibility of locally grown foods. Driving along any road in the height of summer, you are likely to encounter at least one or two roadside farm stands, piled high with fresh products picked that day. Or, if you're lucky, you might stumble upon a more permanent farm store, stocked with meats, dairy, and fresh veggies too. Many local grocery stores also carry a selection of locally grown foods.

If you are new to the world of eating locally and cooking seasonally, it can be overwhelming trying to remember what foods are readily available in each season. Using meats and dairy products, which are available year-round, as a foundation and building your meals from there is a good place to start. This book is organized seasonally in order to help you make the most of each season's ingredients.

Responsibly Sourced Meat and Animal Products

Not all meat is created equal, and there are several important factors to keep in mind when sourcing meat and animal products. It is wonderful to purchase locally grown organic meat from a farm you trust, so that you can be confident that the farmers are using sustainable farming practices and are producing a high quality product. But sometimes these products can be prohibitively expensive. A more cost effective option can be buying a meat share from a local farm. Many farms offer lower prices if you purchase a quarter or half of an animal and pay in advance. If you know that you will be able to use this quantity of meat in a timely manner, look for farms that offer meat by the quarter or half.

Also, look for farms that have a store on the farm. Because these farms are selling their products directly to the consumer, they are often able to cut the price down by eliminating the "middleman," in this case, the grocery store. A visit to a farm is also the perfect opportunity to meet the farmers, and see the place where your food comes from, giving you a closer connection to your food!

Local, fresh eggs are easy to come by, but if you have the time and space, a few backyard chickens could be perfect for you! Backyard chickens are very popular and for good reason—chickens are fun and personable, and they can be more pets than farm animals, of course with the added bonus of fresh eggs!

Finding the right local farm to supply your ingredients can make a big difference in the quality of your food, so it is worth spending the time to find a good source for your meat and other animal products.

The Recipes

Spring

Spring

As winter slowly releases its grip on the sleeping land, tiny green shoots begin to peek through the still cool soil. The earth remains cold, but the sun is strong and warm, and plumes of sweet-smelling steam rise up from sugar shacks perched on distant hillsides. It is at this time of year that spring ephemerals, such as wild leeks and fiddlehead ferns, are often the first green thing available from the local land. Mother nature knows best, and wild edibles beat human grown greens across the finish line every time. But salad greens and kale are not far behind with asparagus right on their heels! The recipes that we have created for this season highlight these early spring flavors that we are all craving after a winter where the only local foods available to us lack this vibrant color and fresh flavor. It is not too long before the later spring crops make their appearance: herbs, sweet and tart rhubarb, and peas. The recipes in this chapter are bright and fresh and highlight all of those fresh early season foods that are so welcome after a cold winter!

Recipe Guide

Shiitake Herb Stuffed Pork Tenderloin

 4–6 servings

 45 minutes

6 strips bacon
1 white onion, finely chopped
2 cups shiitake mushrooms
4–5 cloves garlic, minced
3 tablespoons chopped parsley
1 teaspoon chopped thyme leaves

¼ teaspoon pepper
1 teaspoon salt, divided
¾ cup hard cider
1 pork tenderloin
1 tablespoon ghee

Directions

1. Preheat the oven to 350°F.
2. Cut the bacon into small pieces. Cook the bacon over low-medium heat, stirring frequently until crispy. Remove the bacon from the pan and set aside.
3. In the bacon grease, sauté the chopped onion until translucent.
4. In a food processor, blend the mushrooms, (stems included) until finely chopped. Add the chopped mushrooms to the onions and sauté. Add the garlic, parsley and thyme, black pepper, and ½ teaspoon salt.
5. Add the hard cider, and boil until it has reduced by about ¾ and the mixture has thickened.
6. Prepare the tenderloin while the cider reduces.
7. Slice the tenderloin down the middle, cutting two thirds of the way though. Open it up at the slit. Place the tenderloin between two pieces of plastic wrap. Using a meat tenderizer or similar tool (a rolling pin also works), whack the tenderloin to flatten it.
8. Once flat, generously salt both sides of the meat with the remaining ½ teaspoon of salt.

Continued on the next page...

9. Place the filling on top of the pork and roll it into a log.
10. Tie shut with butcher's twine.
11. Heat a large cast iron skillet over high heat. Melt the ghee into the skillet. Once hot, sear the pork, browning all sides.
12. Place in the oven at 350°F and bake for about 30 minutes until it reaches an internal temperature of 145°F.
13. Remove from the oven and allow to rest for at least 10 minutes before cutting.
14. Slice into rounds and serve.

The truly unique thing about spring in Vermont is that you are working on finishing the last of the storage crops from the previous year, while at the same time beginning to reap the bounty of the year to come. If you're making this recipe in the spring as it's written here, you will likely still be working on last year's storage onions and garlic but using the very first shiitakes of the year. The ingredients of the previous and coming year join together to create this beautiful and delicious pork roast.

Crispy Buttermilk Chicken with Maple Bourbon BBQ Sauce

 4 servings

 3 hours

For the Chicken
2 cups buttermilk
2 teaspoons salt
1 teaspoon black pepper
8 chicken drumsticks
1 cup uncooked polenta
½ teaspoon salt
¼ teaspoon black pepper
1 teaspoon dried chimayo chili, crushed
¼ ghee, melted

For the Barbecue Sauce
½ small white onion
2 cloves garlic
1 cup canned tomato sauce
½ teaspoon salt
2 tablespoons apple cider vinegar
½ cup maple syrup
½ cup bourbon
1 tablespoon dried chimayo chilis or other medium heat chili, finely chopped

Directions

1. First prepare the marinade by mixing together the buttermilk, salt, and black pepper in a large resealable plastic bag. Add the chicken drumsticks to the marinade and place in the refrigerator for at least two hours, or overnight.
2. Preheat the oven to 425°F.
3. Prepare the dredge by mixing together the polenta, salt, black pepper, and dried chimayo chili.
4. Take the drumsticks straight from the marinade into the dredge and coat thoroughly.
5. Once coated in polenta, place drumsticks on a baking tray and drizzle generously with melted ghee.
6. Bake at 425°F for 50 minutes, flipping the drumsticks halfway through.
7. While the chicken is baking, prepare the sauce.

Continued on the next page...

8. Sauté the onion and garlic in a medium saucepan for several minutes, until the onions are lightly browned, then add the canned tomato sauce.
9. Cook over medium heat, until the tomato sauce is reduced by half, so you are left with about ½ cup.
10. Add the salt, apple cider vinegar, maple syrup, bourbon, and chimayo chili to the sauce and bring to a boil. Remove from heat.
11. Blend the sauce until smooth with an immersion blender or food processor.
12. To serve, drizzle the chicken with the spicy maple bourbon barbecue sauce.

While it is certainly possible to grow grains such as wheat and oats in Vermont, it is logistically challenging for a small home gardener, and locally grown grains are not easy to find. This is why we have steered away from using these ingredients, and instead opted for a polenta breading for our crispy buttermilk fried chicken. Polenta is versatile and underrated, offering different complex flavors and textures, and dry corn is easy to grow and grind at home! Don't even get me started on the maple bourbon barbecue sauce — we all know just how delicious maple and bourbon are together, and beyond that, I will let this sauce speak for itself!

Lamb Meatballs With Tzatziki

 4 servings   1 hour

For the Meatballs
1 tablespoon chopped fresh parsley
½ tablespoon chopped fresh mint
2 tablespoon chopped chives
1 tablespoon chopped fresh oregano
1 small red onion, finely diced
2 cloves garlic, minced
1 pound ground lamb
1 teaspoon salt
¼ teaspoon black pepper
To Serve
Feta cheese

For the Tzatziki
1 cup yogurt
1 clove garlic, minced
1 tablespoon apple cider vinegar
1 tablespoon chopped dill
1 tablespoon chopped parsley
1 tablespoon chopped mint
2 tablespoons chopped chives
2 tablespoons chopped oregano
1 tablespoon olive oil
¼ teaspoon salt

Directions

1. Preheat the oven to 400°F.
2. To make the meatballs, start by finely chopping all the herbs.
3. Finely dice the red onion and mince the garlic.
4. Mix together the lamb, red onions, garlic, salt, pepper, and herbs.
5. Form into approximately 1½-inch meatballs (makes about 10–12) and place on a greased baking sheet.
6. Bake for 20 minutes at 400°F.
7. While the meatballs bake, prepare the tzatziki by combining all of the ingredients and mixing together well.
8. Serve with tzatziki and crumbled feta.

This recipe is just what you need when you're looking for a change of pace. "Lamb Meatballs with Tzatziki" sounds like the kind of recipe that requires spices from around the world, but this interpretation manages to capture those bold and complex flavors while keeping the seasonings close to home. I love this recipe for a late spring day when the sun is warm and I'm craving a lighter, more refreshing meal. Try this recipe paired with the Parsnip and Sweet Potato Fries (p. 53) and you won't be disappointed!

Herbed Ricotta Stuffed Chicken

 4 servings

55 minutes

1 cup ricotta
1 teaspoon chopped thyme
1 tablespoon chopped oregano
1 tablespoon chopped parsley
2 tablespoon chopped chives
2 cloves garlic, minced
1 tablespoon honey
1 teaspoon salt

¼ teaspoon pepper
1 teaspoon apple cider vinegar
4 large chicken breasts
2 tablespoons ghee
1 onion
1 cup Vermont hard cider
4 slices prosciutto

Directions

1. Preheat the oven to 400°F.
2. Make the herbed ricotta filling by mixing together the ricotta, chopped herbs, minced garlic, honey, salt, pepper, and apple cider vinegar.
3. Make a deep slit in the side of the chicken breast, creating a pocket for the filling.
4. Stuff each chicken breast with a scoop of ricotta filling.
5. Salt both sides of the stuffed chicken breasts.
6. In a cast iron skillet, heat the ghee over a high heat. Sear the chicken breasts on both sides until golden brown.
7. Add in the onion peeled and chopped into thick slices.
8. Pour the apple cider into the pan and bake at 400°F for about 20 minutes until the chicken reaches an internal temperature of 165°F. If you do not have a meat thermometer you can also tell the chicken is done when the juices run clear.
9. While the chicken is cooking, make the crispy prosciutto.
10. Cook the prosciutto over medium heat until the fat renders and it crisps up, very similar to how bacon looks when done.
11. To serve the chicken, garnish with crispy prosciutto and fresh herbs.

This recipe has so much going for it. It is every bit as flavorful as it is simple. This recipe was inspired by the fresh herbs that start to become available in late spring—thyme, oregano, parsley, and chives are the dominant flavors, perfectly balanced by the mild ricotta and chicken flavors. A little bit of crispy fried prosciutto tops the dish off with that salty flavor and a tiny bit of crunch!

Herb Butter Basted Steak

 **4 servings**   **45 minutes**

2 teaspoons salt, divided
Black pepper to taste
4 (6–8 ounces) top round or
sirloin steaks
3 tablespoons chopped parsley
1 tablespoon chopped oregano

1 tablespoon chopped thyme
1 tablespoon chopped winter savory
4–5 cloves garlic, minced
½ cup unsalted butter, softened
½ tablespoon ghee

Directions

1. Generously salt and pepper both sides of the steaks and set aside while you prepare the herb butter.
2. Mix the herbs and garlic together with the butter and ½ teaspoon of salt.
3. Heat a cast iron skillet over high heat with ½ tablespoons of ghee.
4. Once the pan is hot (you can test this by flicking a few drops of cold water into the pan and listening for a sizzle) add the steaks and sear for 1–2 minutes on the first side until golden brown.
5. Flip the steaks and reduce the heat to medium high. Add in a few tablespoons of the herb butter and begin basting the steak, spooning the herb butter over the steak as it cooks.
6. Continue basting the steak, adding more butter when needed until the steak is cooked to your liking. Cook to an internal temperature of 130–135°F for medium rare, 140–145°F for medium, 150–155°F for medium well, and 160°F for well done.
7. Remove the steak from the pan and allow it to rest for about 5 minutes before serving.

It is hard to beat a locally raised, grass fed steak, but add butter with fresh picked herbs and you have found the key to my heart. There is just something about those fresh spring herbs that my taste buds have longed for all winter long, and when parsley, basil, and rosemary become ready in late spring I can't get enough of this herb butter. Fresh herbs are wonderfully easy to grow, whether you have a big home garden or just a window box. Basil, parsley, summer savory, and rosemary take up very little space, and the reward of having fresh herbs at your fingertips makes it a no-brainer.

Savory Polenta Bowl

 4 servings

 30 minutes

For the Crispy Chili Brown Butter Sauce

¾ cup unsalted butter

4–5 cloves garlic, minced

1–2 small shallots, finely chopped

⅛ cup chopped dried chimayo chilis

½ tablespoon salt

1 tablespoon maple sugar

For the Polenta

4 cups water

1 teaspoons salt

1 cup polenta

¼ cup unsalted butter

½ cup grated cheddar cheese

For the Vegetable Topping

1 bunch asparagus (approximately 1 pound)

6 ounces fresh shiitake mushrooms

2 cloves garlic, minced

2 small shallots, minced

½ tablespoon chopped fresh thyme

2–3 tablespoons butter

¾ teaspoon salt

To Serve

2 balls fresh burrata cheese

Directions

1. For the crispy chili brown butter, melt ¾ cup unsalted butter in a small saucepan over low heat.
2. Finely chop the garlic and shallots and add to the melted butter. Increase to medium heat.
3. Let simmer, stirring occasionally until the garlic and shallots are golden and crispy and the butter turns light brown.
4. Remove from the heat, chop the dried chilis, and stir them into the butter mixture along with the salt and maple sugar.
5. Set aside and allow the flavors to infuse while you prepare the vegetables and polenta.
6. For the vegetable mixture, start by preparing your asparagus. Snap the ends of the asparagus off and chop the remaining stalks into 1-inch pieces.

Continued on the next page...

7. Remove the stems from the shiitake mushrooms and discard. Leave the smallest mushroom caps whole and cut the larger ones into quarters so they are all roughly the same size.
8. Mince the garlic, shallots, and thyme.
9. Over medium heat, melt 2–3 tablespoons of butter. Add the shallots and cook for 1–2 minutes until they begin to turn translucent.
10. Add the asparagus and mushrooms, salt and thyme and sauté until the asparagus turns bright green and is tender.
11. Add the garlic and cook for another minute.
12. To make the polenta, bring 4 cups of water and 1 teaspoon of salt to a boil over high heat.
13. Once the water is boiling, add in the polenta and turn the heat down to low. Whisk vigorously for 4–5 minutes over low heat until the polenta starts to thicken.
14. Remove from the heat and stir in the butter and grated cheese until melted.
15. To serve, spoon polenta into a bowl, top with the asparagus and mushroom mixture, ½ of a burrata, and the Crispy Chili Brown Butter Sauce.

Maybe you have never thought of polenta as a breakfast food, and if that is the case you are about to be introduced to a whole new world of breakfast ideas! While this dish could easily be made as lunch or even a light dinner, we designed it with breakfast in mind. Savory breakfast options are way underrated, and I'm always looking for something a little heartier to start my day. Spring veggies top this bowl, fresh asparagus and shiitake mushrooms, but you can experiment with whichever veggies you have available!

Wild Leek and Fiddlehead Soup

 4 servings   **1 hour**

½ white onion
1–2 cloves garlic
1 pound potatoes
2 tablespoons butter
1½ teaspoons salt, divided
3 cups chicken stock

3 cups fiddleheads
3 dozen ramp leaves
½ cup cream
2 tablespoons crème fraiche
½ tablespoon apple cider vinegar

Directions

1. Begin by dicing the onion, mincing the garlic, and peeling and dicing the potatoes.
2. Melt the butter in a large saucepan over medium heat. Add the onions and sauté for 2–3 minutes until translucent. Add the minced garlic and ½ teaspoon of salt.
3. Add the potatoes and chicken stock and bring to a boil.
4. Boil for about 20 minutes until the potatoes are soft.
5. While the potatoes cook, prepare the fiddleheads and ramps. Chop the ramp leaves and set aside. Thoroughly rinse the fiddleheads, making sure the brown papery coating has been removed.
6. Bring several quarts of water to boil in a medium saucepan, boil the fiddleheads for 15 minutes. This is a crucial step that makes fiddleheads safe to eat.
7. After 15 minutes, immediately place the fiddleheads in cold water to stop the cooking process.
8. Once the potatoes are soft, add the chopped ramps, cooked fiddleheads, and cream. Remove from the heat and blend until smooth using an immersion blender.
9. Add the crème fraiche, apple cider vinegar, and the remaining 1 teaspoon of salt. Blend again.
10. To serve, garnish with crème fraiche.

Wild leeks and fiddlehead ferns are ready for harvest at almost exactly the same time, and they even tend to grow in the same places. In other words, having a recipe that combines these two spring wild edibles is a match made in heaven. This soup is warm and comforting, perfect for those spring evenings that still get quite chilly! For an added bonus, if you are still storing a few potatoes from last fall, this recipe is a great way to use them up, even if they aren't as beautiful as they once were!

Asparagus, Burrata, and Pea Salad

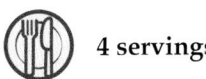 **4 servings**   **35 minutes**

⅓ cup olive oil
3 tablespoons Apple cider vinegar
¼ teaspoon salt, plus more for boiling water
¼ teaspoon pepper
3 tablespoons maple syrup
6–8 sprigs thyme, chopped
½ tablespoon chopped chives

1 teaspoon chopped oregano
2 bunches asparagus
1 cup green peas
1 cup snow peas
4 radishes
16 ounce burrata (2 balls)
4 slices prosciutto

Directions

1. Make the vinaigrette by whisking together the olive oil, apple cider vinegar, salt, pepper, maple syrup, thyme, chives, and oregano. Set aside.
2. Bring a pot of water to a boil and salt generously (about ½ tablespoon of salt per quart of water).
3. Snap the ends off the asparagus and discard. Blanch the asparagus for 3 minutes until bright green and tender, immediately transfer to ice cold water.
4. Blanch the green peas and snow peas for 1 minute, immediately transfer to ice cold water.
5. Slice the asparagus in half lengthwise and mix with the peas. Toss with vinaigrette.
6. Top the salad with thinly sliced radishes, torn burrata, and prosciutto.

Just when you think nothing is as vibrant and green as asparagus, enter fresh peas! This recipe is simple enough to make for a large group, and let me tell you, it is a crowd pleaser! I have always loved asparagus cooked lightly, so it keeps just a bit of crunch, and the creaminess of the burrata nicely balances the fresh snap of the peas and asparagus. Add those salty little bits of prosciutto and you have a seriously unique and tasty salad!

Potato and Wild Leek Gratin

 **8 servings**   **2 hours**

1–2 large cloves garlic, minced
6–8 thyme sprigs
1 cup whole milk
1½ cups cream
1 teaspoon salt
¼ teaspoon black pepper

2½ pounds Yukon Gold potatoes
4 dozen ramps (about 3¼ ounces)
2 tablespoons butter
1½ cups grated extra-sharp cheddar cheese

Directions

1. Preheat the oven to 400°F.
2. Mince the garlic.
3. Add the minced garlic, thyme sprigs, whole milk, cream, salt, and pepper together in a small saucepan and heat until hot but not yet boiling.
4. Once hot, remove the milk mixture from the heat. Allow the garlic and thyme flavors to infuse into the milk while you prepare the potatoes and ramps. Once infused, remove the thyme sprigs.
5. Peel the potatoes and slice into thin slices, do NOT rinse the potatoes or put them in cold water once cut, as you want the extra starch to help bind the layers together.
6. Chop the ramps into 1-inch pieces.
7. Melt the butter in a large saucepan or cast-iron skillet over medium high heat and sauté the ramps until just cooked. They will soften and turn a bright green color when done.
8. To assemble the gratin, start by spooning a little of the milk mixture into the bottom of your 10-inch cast iron skillet.
9. Set aside ¼ cup of cheese to top the gratin with at the end.

Continued on the next page...

10. Begin with one layer of potatoes, followed by a layer of cooked ramps and a sprinkle of cheddar, and cover with more of the milk mixture.
11. Repeat this process until the pan is full.
12. Bake uncovered at 400°F for 1–1½ hours, until the top is golden brown, and the potatoes are soft all the way through.
13. To finish, sprinkle the remaining ¼ cup of grated cheese on top of the gratin and place the dish under the broiler on high for 2–3 minutes until the cheese browns.
14. Serve hot.

I have always loved the combination of potatoes and garlic or potatoes and leeks, but potatoes and wild leeks combined are exponentially better! Wild leeks just have that extra bit of kick, a bit more flavor than anything else, and their short season makes them even more of a treat. Of course, you can absolutely make this recipe using farm grown leeks or even scallions if that is what you have available, and it will still be delicious—there's no way that the potato, cheese, leek combo could ever be bad—but if you can get your hands on the real thing, the wild leeks, it's worth the trouble!

Honey Butter Radishes with Whipped Feta

 4–6 servings

 1 hour 10 minutes

For the Radishes
2 pounds red radishes
3 tablespoons butter
2 tablespoons honey
½ teaspoon salt
¼ teaspoon pepper
10 sprigs thyme, chopped

For the Whipped Feta
6 ounces feta cheese
¼ cup yogurt
⅛ teaspoon salt
⅛ teaspoon pepper
1 tablespoon honey
1 clove garlic

Directions

1. Preheat the oven to 400°F.
2. Remove the tops and tips from the radishes.
3. Melt the butter, then toss the radishes together with the melted butter, honey, salt, pepper, and thyme.
4. Spread the radishes on a baking sheet and bake for 45–50 minutes, stirring occasionally, until soft.
5. While the radishes roast, prepare the whipped feta.
6. In a food processor, place the feta, yogurt, salt, pepper, honey, and garlic together. Blend until combined.
7. Serve the roasted radishes with the whipped feta on top.

Radishes are one of the easiest things to grow, and one of the earliest vegetables ready for harvest in the early days of spring. After a long winter of hearty storage crops the first radishes are a sign of spring, and of the bounty of fresh produce that is to come. Often, radishes are used as a garnish, tossed haphazardly onto a salad, but this recipe makes the radishes the star of the show, celebrating the first fresh produce the year has to offer.

Parsnip and Sweet Potato Oven Fries

 4–6 servings

 1 hour

4 large parsnips
3 large sweet potatoes
3 tablespoons ghee, melted
1 teaspoon salt

1 clove garlic, minced
5–8 sprigs thyme
6 sprigs rosemary

Directions

1. Preheat the oven to 400°F.
2. Peel the parsnips and sweet potatoes and chop them into long sticks.
3. Toss the parsnips and sweet potatoes together with the melted ghee, salt, minced garlic, and whole sprigs of thyme and rosemary. Spread evenly across two baking trays in a single layer.
4. Bake for 20–40 minutes. (20 minutes for just cooked, closer to 40 if you prefer your fries brown and slightly crispy.)

If you think French fries are your favorite food, you have to try Sweet Potato and Parsnip Oven Fries! This recipe is simple and quick, perfect for a weeknight dinner, and so tasty that even picky eaters are sure to dig in! Sweet potatoes and parsnips are both early spring staples, as they can be stored for many months without losing quality.

Asparagus and Goat Cheese Frittata

 6–8 servings

 1 hour 15 minutes

1–2 tablespoons butter
1 medium onion
2 cloves garlic, minced
1½ teaspoon salt, divided
1 bunch asparagus
5 ounces spinach

1 cup grated cheddar cheese
9 eggs
¾ cup whole milk
¼ teaspoon black pepper
4 ounces chèvre

Directions

1. Preheat the oven to 350°F.
2. Melt the butter in a medium cast iron skillet over medium heat. Sauté the onions and garlic together for a few minutes until they begin to turn translucent. Then add ½ teaspoon of salt.
3. Break the ends off of the asparagus and cut the stalks into 1-inch pieces.
4. Add in the asparagus and sauté for another 5 minutes until the asparagus is cooked.
5. Set aside 1 handful of raw spinach for the top, then add in the remaining spinach and cook until wilted.
6. Remove from the heat and stir in the grated cheddar cheese.
7. Whisk together the eggs, milk, black pepper, and the remaining 1 teaspoon of salt.
8. Pour the egg mixture over the vegetables.
9. Top with a handful of raw spinach and crumbled chèvre.
10. Bake at 350°F for 40–45 minutes.

A frittata is one of the most versatile dishes out there; you can interpret it in so many ways and fill it with so many incredible different flavors. Staying true to the ingredients available in spring, I filled this frittata with spinach and asparagus, two staples of early spring and two of the first veggies to become ready here in Vermont. Spinach and asparagus both have a slight sweetness to them, and the tart goat cheese nicely balances this out. Add in a zingy bite of garlic and this recipe is a winner!

Hashbrown Eggs Benedict

 2 servings

 30 minutes

For the Hashbrowns
1 pound potatoes (about 3 cups grated)
1 egg
1 teaspoon salt
2 cloves garlic
2–3 tablespoons butter

For the Poached Eggs
4 eggs
1 teaspoon apple cider vinegar

For the Hollandaise
½ cup butter, melted
3 egg yolks
¼ teaspoon salt
½ teaspoon apple cider vinegar
2 teaspoons water

To Serve
4 strips bacon
5 ounces spinach
2 tablespoons butter
¼ teaspoon salt

Directions

1. Start by making the hashbrowns. Peel and grate the potatoes and place in a bowl. Do not rinse the potatoes as the natural starch will help the hash brown patties hold together.
2. Mix egg, salt, and garlic into the grated potatoes.
3. In a large cast iron skillet, heat 2–3 tablespoons of butter over medium heat. Form the grated potato mixture into patty shapes, about 3 inches in diameter. Once the butter is melted and the pan is hot, place the patties into the skillet 2–3 at a time.
4. Fry in butter for 5–6 minutes per side until the patties are golden brown and hold together.
5. Set the hashbrowns aside and prepare bacon and spinach.
6. Cook the bacon over medium heat until crispy. Set aside.
7. Sauté the spinach in butter, adding the salt at the end. Set aside.
8. Next, prepare the hollandaise. Melt the butter and set aside to cool slightly. As the butter cools the milk solids will float to the top. Scrape off any milk solids that have separated and discard them, so you are left with clarified butter.

Continued on the next page...

9. Bring a pot of water to a gentle simmer. Place a glass bowl over the pot ensuring the water does not touch the bottom of the bowl.
10. Place the egg yolks in the glass bowl. Begin slowly pouring the melted butter into the egg yolks, whisking the entire time. It is important to pour the butter in very slowly and make sure it is fully incorporated before adding more so the mixture does not split.
11. Once all the butter is incorporated, add the salt, apple cider vinegar, and water and whisk until combined. Turn the burner off, but leave the glass bowl containing the sauce over the hot water. Cover and leave sitting over the warm water while you poach the eggs.
12. Bring a small saucepan of water to a boil and add ½ teaspoon of vinegar. Swirl the water with a spoon and crack the egg into the middle of the pot. The swirling water will help the egg whites wrap around the yolk, giving you a neater poached egg.
13. Simmer for 2–4 minutes, then scoop the egg out. Repeat this with the other eggs.
14. To assemble, place the spinach on top of the hashbrowns, followed by the bacon. Place the poached eggs on top and cover with hollandaise sauce.

Just when I thought eggs Benedict couldn't get any better, I tried it served over hashbrowns—talk about a game changer! This recipe combines what might just be the two most delicious breakfast foods ever made—crispy browned potatoes and poached eggs, topped with that silky smooth hollandaise. This one will really fill you up too, making it the perfect breakfast for a big day!

Fresh Green Shakshuka

 4–6 servings

30 minutes

1 bunch asparagus (about 1 pound)
1 small white onion
2 cloves garlic, minced
2–3 tablespoons butter
1 cup green peas
½ pound spinach

½ bunch cilantro
½ cup cream
1 teaspoon salt
¼–½ cup water
6 eggs

Directions

1. Bring a pot of salted water to a boil (about 1 tablespoon salt per quart of water) to blanch the veggies.
2. Snap the ends off of the asparagus and discard. Chop into 1-inch pieces and set the tips aside. Slice the white onion.
3. In a frying pan, melt the butter and sauté the onion, minced garlic, asparagus tips, green peas, and half of the spinach until cooked through.
4. While the veggies sauté, blanch the remaining asparagus stalks and spinach. Blanch the asparagus for 2–3 minutes, and transfer to a food processor. Blanch the spinach for 30 seconds and transfer to a food processor. Add the raw cilantro, cream, and salt to the food processor and blend.
5. Add the sauce to the frying pan and stir together with a ¼ to ½ cup of water.
6. Over medium heat, crack the eggs into the shakshuka and cover with a lid. Allow the eggs to poach in the sauce for 4–6 minutes until cooked through.

This twist on the more traditional tomato-based shakshuka is a perfect, healthy breakfast to start your day. The fresh asparagus, spinach, and peas come together with the herbs to create a thick creamy sauce bursting with flavor. I love this recipe for all of the fresh vegetables that it incorporates. This dish never leaves me wondering if I need to eat more veggies!

Maple Panna Cotta with Rhubarb Compote

 4–6 servings

 20 minutes

2½ teaspoons powdered gelatine
2 tablespoons cold water
1⅔ cups cream
½ cup milk
3 tablespoons maple sugar

For the Rhubarb Compote
1 cup rhubarb, chopped
1 tablespoon maple sugar
2 tablespoons water

Directions

1. In a small bowl, sprinkle the gelatine over the cold water and set aside to let bloom.
2. Gently heat cream, milk, and maple sugar together over a low heat, stirring occasionally. Heat until the milk mixture begins to steam, and the maple sugar is dissolved.
3. Remove the milk mixture from the heat and stir in the bloomed gelatine, making sure the gelatine is completely dissolved and there are no clumps.
4. Pass the mixture through a fine sieve to make sure there are no clumps.
5. Pour the mixture into 4-ounce jelly jars, or any small dish of your choosing, and place uncovered in the refrigerator to set.
6. Place the chopped rhubarb, maple sugar, and water together in a small saucepan over low heat.
7. Allow the mixture to simmer for 10 minutes, stirring occasionally.
8. Allow the mixture to cool completely before topping the panna cottas.
9. Once set, top the panna cottas with the rhubarb and serve.

Thinking of ways to use rhubarb can be tough. Of course, you can make the classic rhubarb pie or crumble, but rhubarb is so abundant you just can't use it all up in a pie. This recipe isn't going to use it all either, but it will help, and it is just delicious! The tart flavor of the rhubarb perfectly balances the sweet maple panna cotta. This is a great make-ahead dessert, as the panna cotta can be kept in the fridge for several days. If you're making these ahead, simply wait to add the rhubarb topping until you are ready to serve!

Summer

Summer

By the time spring turns to summer, the days are long, and the landscape is bright green, each distant hill looking like a giant head of broccoli with varying shades of color and texture. During the heat of the day, a humid haze settles over the valleys and only atop the mountains does the air remain fresh and crisp. The days are warm, and the evenings are long and slow, setting summer in our memories with a nostalgic feel. It is in the early summer when you swear that you can hear plants growing and it is at this time of year that the bounty begins! Early summer starts with bright green broccoli and crunchy carrots and the eager anticipation of the sweet midsummer tomatoes, peppers, corn, and summer squash.

But summer happens fast, and in a matter of weeks, tomatoes and zucchini, once longed for, become overly abundant and even cast aside in the chaos of the season. At this time of year, you can't drive far without passing a farmers market or roadside farmstand, overflowing with the summer's bounty, and even the local grocery stores look just a bit more colorful with local produce on their shelves! Our summer recipes highlight the fleeting flavors of the summer months, combined with some meat and dairy products to create meals that capture the essence of summer in Vermont.

Recipe Guide

Cousin Sarah's Crispy Corn Cakes

 4 servings

 30 minutes

For the Corn Cakes
1 cup unsalted butter, divided
1 cup water
2 cups cornmeal
2½ teaspoons salt
¼ teaspoon black pepper
½ jalapeno, finely chopped (optional)
2 ears corn, cut off the cob

For the Toppings
2 ears of corn
1 pint cherry tomatoes
4–6 scallions
1 medium red onion
2 jalapeno peppers, optional
1 bunch cilantro
4 ounces feta cheese
2 cups cooked black beans

Directions

1. Place ½ cup of the butter and the water in a small saucepan and bring to a boil.
2. Stir the salt, black pepper, jalapeno, and fresh corn into the cornmeal. Stir the hot water and butter mixture into the cornmeal until well combined. Set aside to allow the cornmeal to absorb the water while you prepare the toppings.
3. Next, prepare the toppings.
4. Blacken the corn on the grill on high heat or in a cast iron skillet, allow it to cool and cut the kernels off the cob
5. Cut the cherry tomatoes in half and blacken in a cast iron skillet on high heat.
6. Dice the scallions and red onion.
7. Thinly slice the jalapeno if using.
8. Roughly chop the cilantro.
9. Crumble the feta.
10. Once the toppings are prepared, fry the corn cakes.
11. Melt 1 tablespoon of butter in a large cast iron skillet over medium heat.

Continued on the next page...

12. Scoop ⅛ the of the batter at a time into the hot skillet, similar to how you would make a pancake.
13. Fry each cake in butter, adding more butter to the pan when needed until the cake is golden brown (about 2 minutes per side).
14. Top the corn cakes with beans, charred corn, blackened tomatoes, red onion, scallions, jalapenos, and cilantro and serve.

Traditionally a Southern recipe, our cousin Sarah's corn cakes find themselves right at home in the northeast. A few years ago, my cousin introduced me to the idea of corn cakes on a family camping trip and I couldn't get enough of it. Since then, corn cakes have become a summer staple in our house whenever we're looking for an easy dinner! I love that this recipe will never get boring, because the toppings are a little bit different every time I make it.

Brown Butter Cauliflower with Roasted Red Pepper Sauce

 6–8 servings   **50 minutes**

For the Roasted Red Pepper Sauce
2 fresh tomatoes
4 red bell peppers
6 cloves garlic
1 chimayo chili
4 teaspoons apple cider vinegar
2 teaspoons maple syrup
2 teaspoons salt
⅛ teaspoon black pepper

For the Cauliflower
1 large cauliflower
1 tablespoon ghee, melted
¼ teaspoon salt
⅛ teaspoon black pepper
½ cup salted butter
½ cup toasted pumpkin seeds

Directions

1. Preheat the oven to 400°F.
2. Start by preparing the ingredients for the roasted red pepper sauce.
3. Cut the tomatoes in half and remove the seeds. Place face down on a baking sheet along with the whole bell peppers.
4. Bake for 35–40 minutes, turning the peppers over halfway through. The skins will start to blacken in places.
5. While the tomatoes and peppers roast, begin prepping the cauliflower, by cutting it into 2-inch florets.
6. Toss the florets with melted ghee, salt, and pepper and spread evenly across a baking sheet. Bake at 400°F for 20–25 minutes.
7. When the peppers and tomatoes have finished roasting, remove them from the oven and place a glass container over the peppers to trap the steam. Leave them covered for about 10 minutes. This will make the peppers easier to peel.
8. Peel the peppers and remove the seeds.

Continued on the next page...

9. Place the roasted red peppers, roasted tomatoes, garlic, chimayo chili, apple cider vinegar, maple syrup, salt, and black pepper in a food processor and blend until smooth. Set aside the sauce while you prepare the brown butter.

10. Place the butter in a small saucepan over medium to high heat. Stir occasionally until the butter turns a deep golden-brown color. Remove from heat.

11. To serve, spoon the Roasted Red Pepper Sauce into the bottom of a dish. Place the roasted cauliflower onto the layer of sauce and spoon the brown butter over the cauliflower. Top with toasted pumpkin seeds.

When you're looking for a simple recipe that looks beautiful on a plate, look no further. The Brown Butter Cauliflower is light enough to be served as a dinner appetizer, or on its own as a light lunch. One of my favorite things about cauliflower is how mild it is, making it very versatile, and in this case, the mildness of the cauliflower allows the flavor of the browned butter and red pepper sauce to shine through.

Black Bean Falafel
with Beet Hummus

 4–5 servings

 1 hour 45 minutes

For the Falafel
6 cloves garlic
3 small shallots
½ bunch cilantro
1 bunch parsley
½ jalapeno, seeds removed
1 teaspoon salt
3 cups cooked black beans
1 egg

Garden Salsa
1½ pounds tomatoes, diced
1 small red onion, diced
1 clove garlic, minced
½ jalapeno, seeds removed, minced
½ teaspoon salt
1 tablespoon cilantro, chopped

Quick Pickles
½ cup apple cider vinegar
⅓ cup water
2 teaspoons salt
2 tablespoon maple syrup
½ red onion, sliced
2 cucumbers, thinly sliced

Beet Hummus
1 large beet (about 8 ounces)
⅓ cup toasted pumpkin seeds
1½ cups cooked white beans
2 cloves garlic
¾ teaspoon salt
¼ teaspoon black pepper
¼ cup olive oil

Directions

1. Preheat the oven to 400°F.
2. Roasting the beets for the hummus takes a long time, so get them started first. Peel the beets and chop into eighths. Oil and salt the beets and place in a glass dish covered in foil. Bake at 400°F for 1 hour.
3. While the beets roast, prepare the falafel mixture. Place the garlic, shallots, cilantro, parsley, jalapeno, and salt in a food processor and blend until everything is finely chopped.

Continued on the next page...

75

4. Add the black beans and egg and blend until a sticky paste forms with some larger chunks of bean still visible.
5. Form balls with the mixture using about 3 tablespoons of mixture per ball. Place the balls onto a baking sheet lined with parchment paper.
6. Bake at 400°F for 30–35 minutes.
7. While the falafel bakes, prepare the other components.
8. To prepare the quick pickles, in a small saucepan add the apple cider vinegar, water, salt, and maple syrup and bring to a boil. Pour the hot liquid over the sliced red onion and cucumber. Set aside and allow the pickling liquid to infuse while you prepare the salsa and beet hummus.
9. For the garden salsa, mix together the diced tomatoes, diced red onion, minced garlic, minced jalapeno, salt, and chopped cilantro.
10. For the beet hummus, place the pumpkin seeds into a food processor and blend until smooth. Add the cooked beets, cooked white beans, garlic, salt, black pepper, and olive oil and blend until smooth.
11. Serve in a bowl with generous portions of the falafel, pickles, garden salsa, and beet hummus.

The black bean falafel is a really nice vegetarian option with plenty of protein, so it is very filling. The color of the beet hummus is a showstopper, and the flavor of the quick pickles is just as bold! All these dishes combined with a garden salsa makes for a beautifully colorful plate and a mix of flavors that are fresh and memorable!

Savory Pork Stuffed Peppers

 4–6 servings   35 minutes

2 pounds ground pork
6–8 cloves garlic, minced
1 teaspoon chopped thyme
1 tablespoon chopped sage
1 tablespoon chopped summer savory
1 tablespoon chopped oregano
2 tablespoons chopped parsley
1 teaspoon salt

¼ teaspoon pepper
3 tablespoons ghee, divided
2 medium onions, sliced
2 cups sliced shiitake mushrooms
½ cup tomato sauce
6 bell peppers
1 cup grated cheddar cheese

Directions

1. Preheat the oven to 350°F.
2. Mix together the ground pork with the minced garlic, herbs, salt, and pepper.
3. Melt 2 tablespoons of ghee in a large skillet over high heat. Once hot, add the pork and cook, stirring occasionally. It is best to cook the meat in two batches so that it can all have contact with the pan and will brown better and cook faster.
4. Once cooked, remove the meat from the pan and add the remaining ghee and the sliced onions. Sauté for 1–2 minutes, then add the mushrooms. Sauté another 3–4 minutes until the mushrooms are fully cooked. Once cooked, add the pork back to the pan and add the tomato sauce. Remove from heat.
5. Cut the tops off the bell peppers and remove the seeds.
6. Stuff each pepper full to the top with the pork mixture.
7. Cover with foil and bake at 350°F for 45 minutes to 1 hour until the peppers are soft. Remove the foil from the top.
8. Top peppers with cheese and broil on high for 2–3 minutes until the cheese is brown and bubbling. Serve.

These stuffed peppers are a crowd pleaser, and easy to make ahead of time. Melt-in-your-mouth slightly browned cheese covers the beautifully seasoned sausage filling, all encased in a soft, sweet baked pepper. This filling, healthy, delicious dinner is perfect to come home to after a long hot summer day.

Tangy Herb and Yogurt Chicken

 4–6 servings

 3 hours 45 minutes

4 cloves garlic
1 bunch parsley
8–10 sprigs oregano
8–10 sprigs thyme
8–10 sprigs summer savory
1 tablespoon apple cider vinegar
2 teaspoon salt
½ teaspoon black pepper
2 tablespoons maple syrup
1 cup yogurt

2 pounds boneless chicken thighs (about 8 thighs)

For the Garlic Basil Sauce
2 cloves garlic
2 cups basil leaves
½ teaspoon salt
1 teaspoon apple cider vinegar
½ cup olive oil

Directions

1. Make the marinade by combining the garlic, parsley, oregano, thyme, summer savory, apple cider vinegar, salt, pepper, and maple syrup in a food processor and blend until everything is finely chopped. You can keep the stems on the herbs and blend it all together.
2. Add the chopped herbs from the food processor and the yogurt into a large zip lock bag. Add the chicken thighs to the bag, mixing well and sealing carefully.
3. Place the bag in a refrigerator and marinate for at least 3 hours (overnight is best).
4. When the chicken has marinated, preheat the grill to medium-high.
5. Grill the chicken until it reaches an internal temperature of 165°F.
6. While the chicken is on the grill, prepare the Garlic Basil Sauce by placing all the ingredients in a food processor and blending until smooth.
7. Drizzle the chicken with basil sauce and serve.

I'm always looking for different ways to add flavor to chicken. Because chicken itself has such a mild flavor, you can really take it in any direction you want, and this recipe is herby, delicious, and light enough to enjoy on the hottest summer afternoon. The garlic and basil sauce gives the chicken a lovely green color that you will only be able to enjoy in the height of summer, so don't take it for granted. The flavor is all around delicious.

High Summer Steak Kebabs

 4 servings

 2 hours 45 minutes

4 cloves garlic
1 bunch parsley
4–5 sprigs summer savory
1½ teaspoons salt
1 tablespoon apple cider vinegar
⅓ cup olive oil
1 pound sirloin steak

2 bell peppers
1 medium zucchini
1 medium summer squash
12–16 shiitake mushrooms
1 medium red onion

Directions

1. To make the marinade, combine the garlic, parsley, summer savory, salt, apple cider vinegar, and olive oil in a food processor and blend until smooth.
2. Cut the steak into 1-inch cubes and marinate in the refrigerator for at least 2 hours or overnight. It works best to put everything in a large resealable plastic bag.
3. Once the steak has finished marinating, prepare the kebabs.
4. Cut the bell peppers, zucchini, summer squash, mushrooms, and red onion into roughly 1-inch pieces.
5. Skewer a mixture of all the vegetables and steak on each skewer.
6. Grill, over medium high heat, turning the kebabs every few minutes, until the edges are browned, and the steak reaches an internal temperature of 145°F.

You can tell a lot about a person based on what they put on their kebabs! Really! A kebab can be almost anything, making it a great form of culinary self expression! For this recipe, we went the simple route, because more often than not, simple is better, and if you're using the best quality local ingredients there is no need to hide the flavors under a million different spices! These kebabs feature sirloin steak as the main protein, complemented by bell peppers, shiitake mushrooms, summer squash, and red onion.

Garlic and Herb Caprese Salad

 4 servings

 40 minutes

For the Herb Oil
½ cup olive oil
5 cloves garlic, minced
½ teaspoon finely chopped jalapeno
2 tablespoons chopped fresh parsley
1 tablespoon chopped fresh oregano
½ tablespoon chopped fresh rosemary
½ tablespoon chopped fresh summer savory
½ teaspoon salt
¼ teaspoon black pepper

For the Salad
3 large tomatoes
2 cups cherry tomatoes
12 ounce fresh mozzarella
1 bunch fresh basil, chopped
Flaky sea salt, to taste
Freshly ground black pepper, to taste

Directions

1. First make the fresh herb oil. Heat the olive oil, garlic, and jalapeño together over medium-low heat for about 5 minutes until the garlic begins to turn translucent.
2. Remove from heat and add the freshly chopped herbs, salt, and pepper.
3. Allow to infuse for 5–10 minutes while you prepare the salad.
4. Slice the large tomatoes into ¼ inch thick slices.
5. Cut the cherry tomatoes in half.
6. Cube the mozzarella into ½-inch cubes.
7. Layer the tomatoes, mozzarella, and basil into a bowl and top with black pepper and fresh herb oil.

Although I'm not allowed to pick a favorite, this might be one of my favorite summer recipes. A caprese salad is a classic, and this recipe only deviates from that standard in one way, but it is a big way that reinvents the concept entirely. Instead of a balsamic glaze, we opted for a garlic herb oil. Salty, savory, and a tiny bit spicy, this oil perfectly complements the sweet ripe tomatoes. Make sure to use fresh heirloom tomatoes for the best results, ideally several different colors to get that lovely summer look!

Charred Corn Salad

 4 servings

 35 minutes

8 ears sweet corn
Oil and salt for cooking, to taste
2 red peppers, cut in quarters
with seeds removed
1 pint cherry tomatoes
1 medium red onion, diced
2–3 cloves garlic, minced
2 ounces feta cheese, crumbled
5 scallions, chopped

For the Dressing
⅓ cup olive oil
⅓ cup apple cider vinegar
1 teaspoon salt
⅛ teaspoon black pepper

Directions

1. Preheat the grill to high heat (about 400°F).
2. Husk the corn, then oil and salt the ears. Blacken the outside of each ear on the grill. Once blackened, carefully cut the corn kernels off the cob.
3. Oil and salt the red peppers and grill. Once they are cooked through, remove the seeds and dice the peppers into small pieces.
4. Allow the corn and peppers to cool.
5. Chop the cherry tomatoes into quarters.
6. Dice the red onion and mince the garlic.
7. Make the vinaigrette by whisking together the olive oil, apple cider vinegar, salt, and pepper.
8. Mix together the charred corn, red pepper, tomatoes, red onion, garlic, and vinaigrette.
9. Top with crumbled feta and scallions and serve chilled.

Our summers are fleeting, and you want to enjoy every minute of summer air outdoors! For me, this means grilling as many of our summer meals as possible—not just meat, but veggies, too! Sometimes minding the grill is the perfect excuse to be outdoors enjoying the fresh air. This charred corn salad is easy to make for a crowd, which is a good thing because it is a crowd pleaser! Grilling the ears of corn will bring out so much flavor from the corn, both sweet and savory.

Blackened Peach Salad

 4 servings

 20 minutes

For the Apple Cider Dressing
¾ cup apple cider vinegar
3 tablespoons honey
½ teaspoon salt

For the Salad
2 peaches
1–2 tablespoons olive oil
5 ounces mixed baby greens
½ cup blueberries
2 ounce feta, crumbled

Directions

1. First prepare the apple cider dressing. Combine the apple cider vinegar and honey in a small saucepan and boil over a high heat. Reduce by half (so there is slightly less than ½ cup of liquid remaining) and remove from heat. Stir in salt.
2. Slice the peaches into eighths and coat the slices in oil.
3. Grill the sliced peaches on both sides over high heat until they are lightly blackened.
4. Set the peach slices aside to cool to room temperature.
5. Toss the salad greens in the apple cider dressing.
6. Top with grilled peaches, fresh blueberries, and crumbled feta.
7. Drizzle a bit more apple cider dressing over the top of the salad and serve.

Summer is all about refreshing food that brings together the bright flavors and colors of the season, and that is exactly what this salad does. Peaches have a very short season, and they are infinitely better fresh and locally grown, so I like to use them in as many ways as possible while I have the chance. If you still haven't used up all of your peaches with this recipe, make sure to try the Grilled Peaches with Blackberry Mousse on p. 105!

Brown Butter Green Beans with Crunchy Maple Seeds

 4–6 servings

20 minutes

¼ cup toasted pumpkin seeds
¼ cup sunflower seeds
2 tablespoons maple syrup

½ teaspoon flaky sea salt
½ cup salted butter
1 pound green beans

Directions

1. Bring a pot of salted water to a boil (about ½ tablespoon salt per quart of water).
2. While you wait for the water to boil, prepare the crunchy maple seeds.
3. Place the toasted pumpkin seeds, sunflower seeds, maple syrup, and flaky sea salt in a small frying pan over medium heat. Toast, stirring continuously for 1–2 minutes. Remove from heat and set aside.
4. Next, prepare the brown butter by placing the salted butter in a small saucepan over medium heat. Allow the butter to melt. Keep over the heat, stirring occasionally for about 5–8 minutes until the butter turns a deep golden-brown color. Set aside while you prepare the green beans.
5. Remove the stem end from the green beans and discard. Blanch the green beans in the salted water for 3–4 minutes until they turn bright green and are soft. Remove from the water.
6. To serve, pour the brown butter over the green beans and toss so they are evenly coated. Sprinkle the seeds over the top and serve warm.

What do you do with all of those green beans!? If you get veggies from a CSA or grow your own, then you've probably faced the problem of having more green beans than you know what to do with. Enter our Browned Butter Green Beans. I love bringing this recipe as a contribution when I am a guest at a friend's house. The crunchy maple seeds are unique and delicious, a conversation starter to say the least, and this dish is so easy to make!

Grilled Veggie Summer Salad

 4–6 servings

 30 minutes

4 ears corn
Melted ghee and salt for grilling
3 red peppers
4 small-medium summer squash
1 zucchini
1 eggplant
1 large red onion
6 large shiitake mushrooms
½ bunch fresh basil
1 pint cherry tomatoes

For the Dressing
½ cup buttermilk
3 cloves garlic, minced
½ bunch parsley, finely chopped
¾ cup olive oil
½ teaspoon salt
1 tablespoon maple syrup
2 teaspoons apple cider vinegar

Directions

1. Preheat the grill to a high heat.
2. Remove the husks from the ears of corn. Salt and oil the corn and grill until blackened.
3. Cut the red peppers, summer squash, zucchini and eggplant in quarters and cut the red onion into rounds. Remove the seeds from the red peppers.
4. Oil and salt the red peppers, summer squash, zucchini, eggplant, red onion, and shiitake mushrooms and grill until they are cooked through.
5. Once all the veggies are grilled, chop them into bite sized pieces and place in a large bowl. Then chop the basil and quarter the cherry tomatoes and combine with the chopped veggies.
6. Next, prepare the dressing. Add all the ingredients together and whisk until combined.
7. Pour the dressing over the grilled veggies and mix thoroughly. This salad is best if it's left to marinate for 30 minutes to an hour before serving to allow the veggies to absorb the flavors.
8. Top with fresh basil and serve cold.

I don't know about you, but during the summer months I want to eat as many fresh veggies as I can! Well, this salad features them all! I love to make this recipe for a cook-out or bring it to a mid-summer potluck. It is easy to make a big batch, and I always save a little out for myself to enjoy as leftovers the next day!

Cheesy Zucchini Waffles
with Garden Salsa

 2 servings   **40 minutes**

For the Cherry Tomato Topping
1 pint cherry tomatoes
½ teaspoon salt
2 cloves garlic
1 handful basil, chopped
2 tablespoons olive oil

To Serve
2 tablespoons sour cream
1 tablespoon chopped scallions

For the Waffles
2 medium zucchini (2–3 cups shredded)
1 teaspoon salt
1 cup grated cheddar cheese
2 cloves garlic, minced
1 small red onion, finely chopped
2 eggs
¼ teaspoon black pepper

Directions

1. First, make the cherry tomato topping and set aside to allow flavors to develop.
2. Slice the cherry tomatoes into quarters. Add salt, large chunks of garlic (you will take these out before serving, so make sure they are large enough that you can see them), chopped basil leaves, and olive oil. Stir together and set aside while you prepare the waffles.
3. For the waffles, grate the zucchini and add 1 teaspoon of salt. Allow to sit for 5 minutes so the salt will draw the moisture out of the zucchini.
4. Squeeze the shredded zucchini through a muslin cloth or a dish towel to get rid of any excess moisture.
5. Grate 1 cup of Vermont cheddar cheese and add to the shredded zucchini along with the garlic, red onion, eggs, and black pepper. Stir to combine.
6. Place ½ cup of the batter into the center of a preheated and oiled waffle maker.

Continued on the next page...

7. Let the waffle cook for 5–6 minutes until browned. This may be longer than a regular waffle takes, so set a timer rather than relying on the light on the waffle maker.
8. To serve, top the waffles with the Cherry Tomato Topping, a dollop of sour cream and scallions. (Remember to remove the chunks of garlic from the Tomato topping.)

Every home gardener is desperate to get rid of zucchini and summer squash come mid-summer, and this recipe will help you with that task! These zucchini waffles are made in a waffle maker, so that they have the traditional waffle look, but their flavor is savory, and they make a great healthy breakfast option! These waffles are simple, made with zucchini, cheese, eggs and a few other things, but they fill you right up and stick with you all morning, which is a must for breakfast in my opinion.

Sweet Potato Hash Browns with Black Bean Salsa

 3-4 servings

 45 minutes

For the Hashbrowns
1½ pounds sweet potato
4 cloves garlic, minced
1 teaspoon salt
¼ teaspoon black pepper
2 eggs
2–3 tablespoons unsalted butter

To Serve
2 tablespoons butter
4 eggs
Salt to taste

For the Black Bean Salsa
2 ears corn
¼ cups cooked black beans
8 ounces cherry tomatoes, quartered
1 small red onion, diced
1 tablespoon chopped cilantro
2 cloves garlic, minced
1 tablespoon apple cider vinegar
¾ teaspoons salt
¼ teaspoon black pepper

Directions

1. Begin by preparing the sweet potato hash browns. Peel and grate the sweet potatoes. Place in a large bowl and add the minced garlic, salt, black pepper, and eggs. Mix thoroughly.
2. Heat a cast iron skillet over medium heat. Add the butter. Once the butter is melted and sizzling, form the sweet potatoes into 3-inch patties and fry. Cook for about 6–8 minutes per side, until they are golden brown, and the patties hold together.
3. While the sweet potato hash browns cook, begin preparing the black bean salsa.
4. Bring a pot of water to a boil and boil the sweet corn for 3–4 minutes. Remove from the water, cool slightly, then cut kernels off the cob.

Continued on the next page...

5. Mix together the sweet corn, cooked black beans, quartered cherry tomatoes, diced red onion, chopped cilantro, minced garlic, apple cider vinegar, salt, and black pepper.
6. When the sweet potato hash browns are done cooking, add more butter to the pan and fry the eggs in your preferred style, adding salt to taste.
7. Serve the hash browns topped with the Black Bean Salsa and fried eggs.

I honestly don't know why sweet potato hash browns aren't a staple in every diner and home kitchen in the country! I'm not saying they're better than a standard hash brown, but they are certainly every bit as delicious, and their sweetness allows them to pair wonderfully with a number of savory breakfast options. I enjoy my sweet potato hash browns served with black bean salsa and fresh eggs, sunny side up, but you can cook your eggs however you prefer. If you are feeling spicy, consider adding a dash of your favorite hot sauce!

Summer Berry Maple Pavlova

 12-14 servings

 3 hours 30 minutes

For the Meringue
6 large egg whites
1 cup maple sugar

For Topping
1 tablespoon maple syrup
1½ cups heavy cream
1–2 cups mixed berries

Directions

1. Preheat the oven to 225°F.
2. Separate the egg whites from the egg yolks and place the whites in a mixing bowl. Discard the yolks or freeze them to use in another recipe. (Try Maple Bourbon Creme Brûlée, p. 123.)
3. In a stand mixer or using an electric beater, begin whisking the egg whites on high speed until they appear frothy, about one minute.
4. Begin to add the maple sugar one tablespoon at a time, making sure each spoonful is fully incorporated.
5. Once all the maple sugar has been added, continue to beat on high speed for 6–8 more minutes until stiff peaks have formed and the meringue is a glossy texture.
6. Line two baking sheets with parchment paper.
7. Scoop the meringue onto the baking sheets, making 12–14 nest-shaped meringues about 3 inches wide with a depression in the middle.
8. Place the meringues in the oven and bake for 3 hours.
9. Turn the oven off. Leave the meringues in the oven to cool, with the oven door cracked. This prevents them from cracking due to sudden temperature changes.
10. Allow to cool in the oven for at least 2 hours.
11. Just before serving, add 1 tablespoon of maple syrup to the whipping cream. Whip until soft peaks form. Then spoon the whipped cream into the meringue nest and top with mixed summer berries.

In the height of summer, with the berry bushes bursting with gleaming fruit, there are a thousand recipes begging to be made. But none is as exciting to me as a fresh summer berry pavlova. For years I would make this recipe in the more traditional fashion, using regular granulated sugar, but the added flavor brought by the maple sugar puts these pavlovas in a league of their own.

Many people never think of putting something like peaches on the grill, but the high heat really does wonders for them. The resulting peaches are not mushy, but just soft enough to melt in your mouth with beautiful, sweet, caramelized edges. I chose to pair the peaches with a black raspberry mousse because the flavors complement each other so beautifully, and so do the colors. After all, we do eat with our eyes. Black raspberries have a short season, so consider freezing some to use later in the summer with this recipe!

Grilled Peaches with Black Raspberry Mousse

 4-6 servings

 30 minutes

Black Raspberry Mousse
2 teaspoon gelatine powder
¼ cup plus 1 tablespoon cold water, divided
1 cup (8 ounces) black raspberries
¼ cup maple sugar
¾ cup heavy cream

For the Grilled Peaches
2 peaches
1 tablespoon maple syrup

Directions

1. Start by making the black raspberry mousse.
2. Sprinkle the gelatine powder over ¼ cup of cold water and set aside to allow the gelatine to bloom.
3. Heat the berries, maple sugar, and 1 tablespoon of water together in a small saucepan over low heat, stirring occasionally until the berries are mostly to broken down (about 15–20 minutes).
4. Push the mixture through a sieve to remove seeds.
5. Add the bloomed gelatine to the berry juice, return the mixture to the saucepan over low heat, and stir until fully dissolved. Set aside to cool to room temperature.
6. Whip the cream to soft peaks.
7. Once the black raspberry mixture is cooled, gently fold in the whipped cream one third at a time.
8. Place in the fridge for 1 hour to allow the mousse to set.
9. Just before serving, cut peaches in half and drizzle with maple syrup. Grill peaches face down for about 10 minutes.
10. Top grilled peaches with the black raspberry mousse and enjoy!

Fall

Fall

Fall itself could almost be divided into two separate seasons. Early fall, or foliage season, where the trees are bright orange, the sun is hot, and the air is crisp, which eventually gives way to stick season in late October. The leaves drop, and the weather takes a turn for the cold and gray days of late fall.

Fall begins with nearly as much abundance as summer, with all of the cold weather crops becoming ready and winter storage crops—squash, potatoes, and cabbage—just behind. But the cooler weather begins to call for a much different kind of cooking, and many of the fall recipes are warm, cozy, and comforting, embodying the slowing down that comes with the season. Fall too is the time when many animals raised for meat are traditionally harvested, adding to the bounty. The recipes in this section celebrate the abundance of fall, the dropping of temperatures, and the shift towards hearty, cold-weather meals!

Recipe Guide

Cider Braised Pork Shoulder

 6–8 servings

 3 hours 25 minutes

Pork shoulder (about 3 pounds)
1 teaspoon salt
2 tablespoons ghee
2 large shallots, diced
2–3 cloves garlic, minced

4–5 sprigs thyme, chopped
1 bulb fennel, quartered
1 cup chicken stock
2–3 cups apple cider
2 apples

Directions

1. Preheat the oven to 325°F.
2. Generously salt the pork shoulder on all sides.
3. Place a Dutch oven over medium-high heat. Melt the ghee in the pot.
4. Sear the pork shoulder for about 2–3 minutes per side until golden brown.
5. Remove the pork shoulder from the Dutch oven and set aside.
6. Place the diced shallots, garlic, thyme, and fennel into the Dutch oven and sauté for about 1 minute.
7. Return the pork shoulder to the Dutch oven and add the chicken stock and apple cider. The shoulder should be just barely covered by the liquid. If it is not covered, add a bit more stock, apple cider, or water.
8. Bring the mixture to a boil. Once boiling, cover with a lid and place in the oven at 325°F for 3 hours.
9. While the pork is in the oven, peel and quarter the apples and remove cores
10. After 2½ hours, add the apples. Cook for the remaining 30 minutes.
11. Serve over mashed potatoes.

This is one of those recipes that you can put in the Dutch oven, walk away and forget about, and then come back a few hours later to a kitchen full of delicious smells and a dinner that's ready to go. Fresh apple cider is only available for a few months out of the year, and you really will taste the difference of a locally pressed fresh cider. Save a glass to enjoy while your dinner cooks!

Apple and Brie Stuffed Chicken

 4 servings

 40 minutes

4 chicken breasts
7 ounces brie cheese
2 small Pink Lady apples

1 teaspoon salt
1 tablespoon ghee

Directions

1. Preheat the oven to 400°F.
2. Slice the apples into ⅛ inch slices and set aside. Slice the brie into thin slices and set aside.
3. Make a deep slit in the side of the chicken breast, creating a pocket and being careful not to cut all the way through.
4. Generously salt the chicken breasts on all sides.
5. Stuff each chicken breast generously with equal amounts of apple and brie.
6. Use toothpicks to hold the opening of the breast closed so the filling will not fall out while the chicken is cooking.
7. Heat a cast iron skillet over medium to high heat. Melt the ghee in the skillet.
8. Once the skillet is hot, add the chicken breasts and sear for 1–2 minutes per side.
9. Once seared, remove the toothpicks and place the skillet in the oven. Bake at 400°F for about 25–30 minutes or until the chicken reaches an internal temperature of 165°F.
10. Remove from the oven. Some of the brie will have melted out of the chicken as it cooks; spoon the melted brie over the chicken breasts.
11. Allow the chicken to rest for 5 minutes before serving.

Most of us have enjoyed a baked brie as an appetizer at some point, but this brie and apple stuffed chicken takes the idea of baking brie in a different direction. As the chicken cooks, the brie melts, forming a lovely cheese sauce that is complemented by the crispness and sweetness from the apples and the savory flavors from the chicken. Pair it with a nice white wine and you're good to go!

Maple Bourbon Glazed Pork Chops

 4 servings

 **2 hours 20 minutes**

¼ cup maple syrup
¼ cup bourbon
1 tablespoon apple cider vinegar
2 cloves garlic, minced

1½ teaspoons salt, divided
¼ teaspoon black pepper
4 boneless pork chops
1–2 tablespoons ghee

Directions

1. Make the marinade. Combine the maple syrup, bourbon, apple cider vinegar, garlic, ½ teaspoon of salt, and pepper and whisk together.
2. Place the pork chops in a large resealable bag and pour the marinade over them.
3. Marinate pork chops in the refrigerator for at least 2 hours or overnight.
4. Once the pork chops have marinated, preheat the oven to 400°F. Allow pork chops to come to room temperature before cooking.
5. Remove pork chops from marinade and set the marinade aside to be used later. Sprinkle pork chops with 1 teaspoon of salt, salting all sides.
6. Heat a large cast iron skillet over high heat. Add the ghee and let it melt. Once the pan has preheated, sear the pork chops for 2–3 minutes on each side until golden brown.
7. With the pan still over high heat, add the marinade mixture to the pan, allow to bubble and reduce for about 30 seconds before removing from the heat and placing the skillet in the oven.
8. Bake for 10–12 minutes or until the pork reaches an internal temperature of 145°F for medium or 155°F for well done.
9. Spoon the glaze over the pork chops.
10. Allow to rest for 5 minutes before slicing and serving.

This dish takes pork chops to the next level with some of Vermont's most classic flavors as the stars of the show. Sure, I'll sneak maple syrup into a recipe at every chance I can get, but it's the bourbon and apple cider vinegar that cut through the sweetness and balance this dish to perfection. I like to serve these pork chops at almost any occasion with mashed potatoes and roasted vegetables.

Garlic Steak Over Cauliflower Purée

 4 servings

 50 minutes

For the Cauliflower Purée
1 pound cauliflower (about 1 small head)
1 cup cream
1 cup whole milk
2 cloves garlic, minced
1 tablespoon chilled butter, cubed
½ teaspoon salt

For the Steak
4 (8 ounce) New York strip steaks
1 teaspoon salt
1 tablespoon ghee
2 tablespoons butter
2 cloves garlic, whole

For the Chive Garlic Butter
4 tablespoons butter, melted
2 cloves garlic, minced
4 tablespoons chopped chives

Directions

1. Preheat the oven to 400°F.
2. Begin with the cauliflower purée: Chop the cauliflower into small florets and place in a small saucepan.
3. Cover the cauliflower florets in 1 cup of cream and 1 cup of whole milk and add minced garlic.
4. Place the saucepan over medium heat and bring to a boil. Turn the heat down and allow the cauliflower to simmer in the milk and cream mixture for 20 minutes or until soft.
5. Strain the cauliflower, but save the cream and milk mixture and set aside.
6. Place the cauliflower in a food processor or blender along with ¼–½ cup of the reserved cream mixture and purée until smooth. Start by adding ¼ cup of the cream and slowly add more if needed.

Continued on the next page...

7. Add in the chilled butter and salt and continue to puree until smooth. Cover to keep warm while the steaks cook.
8. Next, prepare the steaks. Generously salt both sides of all four steaks. Melt the ghee in a cast iron skillet over high heat. Once the pan has preheated, add the steaks.
9. Sear steaks for about 2–3 minutes on each side. Remove the steaks from the heat and add in butter and garlic cloves. Spoon the butter over the steaks a few times before placing the whole pan in the oven.
10. Bake for about 5 minutes or until a meat thermometer reads 135–140°F for a medium rare steak.
11. Remove steaks from the oven and allow them to rest for about 5 minutes.
12. While the steaks rest, prepare the garlic butter chive sauce. Heat 4 tablespoons of butter over medium heat.
13. Add the minced garlic and sauté for 1 minute. Remove from the heat and add the chopped chives.
14. To serve, spoon cauliflower purée onto plates. Slice the steaks and place the slices on top of the purée, then drizzle with garlic butter sauce.

The sweet cauliflower pairs so nicely with the savory garlic steak and is a perfect way to use your fall cauliflower harvest. This dish is on the fancier side, but truthfully it is not that hard to make. It's all about the elegant presentation. Therefore, this recipe is ideal when you are hoping to impress guests or feel like you deserve a fancy dinner for yourself.

Butternut Squash and Sage Gratin

 6-8 servings

 1 hour

20 sage leaves, divided
5 cloves garlic, minced
1 cup cream
1 cup whole milk
1 large leek
1 medium white onion

2–3 tablespoons butter
1⅛ teaspoon salt, divided
1 large butternut squash
2 cups grated cheddar cheese
¼ teaspoon black pepper

Directions

1. Preheat the oven to 400°F.
2. Finely chop 10 sage leaves (set the other 10 aside for later). Combine the chopped sage, minced garlic, cream, and milk in a small saucepan and warm over low-medium heat. Do not let the mixture boil.
3. While the milk heats, thinly slice the leeks and onions. Melt 1 tablespoon butter in a frying pan and sauté the leeks and onions over low-medium heat until translucent. Stir in ⅛ teaspoon salt.
4. Peel the butternut squash and cut in half lengthwise. Use a spoon to scoop out the seeds. Slice the squash into ⅛ inch thick slices.
5. Set aside ½ cup grated cheese for the top.
6. Begin layering the squash gratin in an 8-inch cast iron skillet.
7. Place a layer of sliced squash and sprinkle it with salt and pepper (you will use about 1 teaspoon of salt and ¼ teaspoon of pepper in total, so roughly divide this amongst the layers.) Next, layer cooked onions and leeks, and cheddar cheese, before spooning ⅓ cup of the cream mixture over the layer.

Continued on the next page...

8. Repeat the layers until your dish is full. Pour any excess cream mixture over the top. Top with the remaining ½ cup of cheddar cheese.
9. Bake at 400°F for 45 minutes to 1 hour until soft when poked with a knife.
10. Just before serving, prepare the crispy sage leaf garnish. Heat 2–3 tablespoons of butter in a small pan over medium heat. Add the remaining 10 sage leaves and fry until crispy.
11. Garnish the gratin with crispy sage leaves and serve.

As Vermont summer rolls into fall, there's a crisp autumn smell in the air, you can see a puff of your breath as you step outside in the morning, and the sunlight dapples through the brightly colored leaves. At this time of year, I begin to crave comfort and coziness. I want nothing more than to curl up with thick wool socks, a warm blanket, and a warm home-cooked meal. This butternut squash gratin is one of those classic comfort foods—it nourishes the body and soul and connects you to that sense of place as the season changes.

Maple Bourbon Crème Brûlée

 4-6 servings

 1 hour 30 minutes

For the Custard
1 cup maple syrup
¼ cup bourbon
2 cups heavy cream
⅛ teaspoon salt
8 egg yolks
1 tablespoon maple sugar

For the Topping
¾ cup maple sugar
3 tablespoons maple syrup

Directions

1. Start by making the custard.
2. Preheat the oven to 325°F.
3. Place the maple syrup into a small saucepan over medium to high heat.
4. When the syrup has reduced down to ¾ of a cup, add the bourbon into the thickened maple syrup. The mixture will bubble a bit as the alcohol burns off.
5. Boil for 2–3 minutes to allow the alcohol to burn off and the mixture to thicken slightly.
6. Stir in the cream and salt and heat until steaming, but do not let the cream boil.
7. While the cream is heating, separate the egg yolks and whisk them together with 1 tablespoon of maple sugar for about 2 minutes until thick.
8. Once the cream is steaming, remove from heat.
9. Pour about ¼ of the cream mixture into the egg yolks and whisk until combined.
10. Slowly pour the remaining cream mixture into the eggs and whisk to combine.
11. Pour the mixture into 4–6 ramekins.
12. Place the ramekins in a baking dish, and pour boiling water into the baking dish until it comes halfway up the sides of the ramekins.
13. Place in the preheated oven and bake for 35–40 minutes.

Continued on the next page...

14. Once baked, allow to cool before adding the topping.
15. To make the topping, mix together the maple sugar and maple syrup.
16. Spread the mixture evenly over the top of each crème brûlée.
17. Holding a blowtorch about three inches above the crème brûlée, and moving constantly, heat the surface of each crème brûlée until the topping bubbles and browns, or even blackens slightly.

There are a lot of recipes out there for maple crème brûlée, but they always seem to be made using a combination of maple sugar and cane sugar, so the maple flavor doesn't come through as much as it could. This crème brûlée uses only maple sugar, even for the crispy brûlée topping, making the maple flavor the star of the show. The complex flavor of the bourbon is subtle, but it does the trick, balancing out the sweetness of the maple. This is hands down the best crème brûlée I have ever had.

Cider and Squash Soup

 4 servings

 1 hour 30 minutes

1 medium butternut squash
2 large carrots
2 small white onions
3–4 cloves garlic
10 sprigs thyme
2 tablespoons ghee, melted
1½ teaspoons salt, divided
¼ teaspoon pepper

¾ cup hard cider
4 cups chicken stock
½ cup crème fraiche

To Garnish
½ cup toasted pumpkin seeds
2 tablespoons crème fraiche

Directions

1. Preheat the oven to 400°F.
2. Peel the butternut squash and carrots and chop into 1-inch cubes.
3. Peel the onions and chop into large chunks.
4. Peel the garlic but leave the cloves whole.
5. Mix together the chopped squash, carrots, onion, garlic cloves, and thyme sprigs. Toss with 2 tablespoons melted ghee, 1 teaspoon salt, and ¼ teaspoon black pepper. Spread across 2 baking sheets and roast at 400°F for 45 minutes.
6. Once roasted, remove the thyme sprigs. Place the remaining ingredients in a medium saucepan over medium heat.
7. Add the hard cider and boil until reduced by ¾. Add the chicken stock and bring to a boil. Add the crème fraiche.
8. Using an immersion blender, blend the soup until smooth. Season to taste.
9. To serve, garnish with crème fraiche and toasted pumpkin seeds.

Squash are ready for harvest mid fall, just in time for colder nights and the perfect soup weather. I love nothing more than a cozy October night with a good book and a bowl of hot soup. This Cider and Squash Soup is so quick and easy, it's the perfect recipe to whip up to satisfy that craving for something warm and comforting.

Broccoli Cheddar Soup

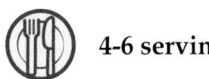 **4-6 servings**

 1 hour

3 small heads broccoli
¾ pound potatoes
2 medium onions
3 tablespoon melted ghee, divided
1½ teaspoon salt, divided
⅛ teaspoon black pepper

4–5 cloves garlic, minced
4–5 sprigs thyme, chopped
4 cups chicken stock
¾ cup cream
2½ cups grated sharp cheddar cheese
¼ cup crème fraiche

Directions

1. Preheat the oven to 400°F.
2. Chop the broccoli into roughly 1-inch pieces. Peel the potatoes and chop into ½-inch cubes. Slice the onions into half inch slices.
3. Toss the chopped broccoli, cubed potatoes, and sliced onions together with 2 tablespoons of melted ghee, ½ teaspoon of salt, and black pepper and spread evenly across a baking sheet.
4. Roast the veggies for 30 minutes or until soft. Set aside about ½ cup of roasted broccoli florets to top the soup.
5. Melt 1 tablespoon of ghee in a saucepan over medium heat. Add in the minced garlic and chopped thyme leaves, and sauté for about 30 seconds until fragrant.
6. Add in the roasted vegetables and chicken stock and bring to a boil. Once the soup reaches a boil, add in the cream, grated cheese, crème fraiche, and remaining salt, and remove from heat.
7. Using an immersion blender, blend the soup until smooth. Add the remaining teaspoon of salt.
8. To serve, top with roasted broccoli florets and grated cheddar cheese.

Vermont is famous for its artisan cheese, and I absolutely love to enjoy said cheese melted into a delicious bowl of broccoli soup. As the summer days transition into fall and the temperatures drop, it is almost fair to call this time of year "soup season," because the weather is just perfect for a hot bowl of soup. Broccoli can be harvested late into the fall in Vermont, being one of the most cold-hardy vegetables, so you can make this recipe with delicious fresh heads of broccoli! Top it with a little bit of extra grated cheese and you will have the whole family coming back for seconds.

Loaded Twice Baked Potatoes

 4-6 servings

 1 hour 40 minutes

8 medium potatoes
1–2 tablespoons ghee
2 medium onions, sliced
2–3 cloves garlic, minced
8 ounces bacon

¼ cup crème fraiche
2 cups grated cheddar cheese
½ cup chopped chives
½ cup cream
¾ teaspoon salt

Directions

1. Preheat the oven to 400°F.
2. Wash the potatoes, leaving the skins on. Prick the skin of each potato with a fork in several places — this allows steam to escape when baking and prevents the potato from bursting. Place the potatoes on a baking sheet and bake for 1 hour or until soft when poked with a fork.
3. While the potatoes bake, prepare the filling. Melt the ghee in a frying pan over low to medium heat. Add the onions and cook, stirring occasionally until caramelized. Once caramelized, stir in the minced garlic and remove from heat.
4. In another skillet, cook the bacon over low heat until crispy. When cooked, chop into small pieces.
5. When fully cooked, remove the potatoes from the oven.
6. Cut the top off each potato longways. Scoop out the inside of the potatoes using a spoon and place in a large bowl. Set aside ½ cup of the grated cheese. Then add the remaining ingredients (caramelized onions, bacon, crème fraiche, 1½ cups cheddar cheese, chives, cream, and salt) to the potato insides and mix well.
7. Add the mixture back into the potato shells and top with the remaining ½ cup of grated cheese.
8. Place back in the oven and bake for 15 minutes or until the cheese is melted and the potatoes are warmed through.

What's better than baked potatoes? A twice baked potato! Pack them full of farm fresh toppings like Vermont cheddar, bacon and sour cream and this is as good as it gets. Everyone loves potatoes, and I have never had someone pass on one of these — even kiddos can't get enough!

Maple Roasted Carrots

 4 servings

 40 minutes

1½ pounds carrots
2 tablespoons butter
2 tablespoons maple syrup
½ teaspoon salt

⅛ teaspoon pepper
2 cloves garlic, minced
10 sprigs thyme
4 sprigs rosemary

Directions

1. Preheat the oven to 425°F.
2. Cut the carrots into quarters lengthwise, to make long, thin carrot sticks.
3. In a small saucepan, combine the butter, maple syrup, salt, and pepper.
4. Toss the carrots in the butter maple sauce and add minced garlic, thyme, and rosemary.
5. Spread evenly across two trays.
6. Bake at 425°F for 20 minutes.
7. Remove the rosemary and thyme and serve warm.

Sweet and crunchy, these maple roasted carrots are like candy. I like to pair them with a salty and savory main course, offering a nice balance between sweet and savory. Carrots store well, so this dish can be made deep into the late fall. When roasting, make sure that the carrots are nice and brown to get that chewy, caramelized glaze.

Crispy Smashed Brussels Sprouts

 2-4 servings

 1 hour 10 minutes

1½ pounds Brussels sprouts
1–2 tablespoons ghee, melted
½ teaspoon salt

¼ teaspoon black pepper
¼ cup fresh grated parmesan cheese
8 strips bacon

Directions

1. Preheat the oven to 400°F.
2. Bring a pot of salted water to a boil (about 1 tablespoon salt per quart of water) to blanch the Brussels sprouts.
3. Cut the ends off the Brussels sprouts and remove any yellow or brown outer leaves.
4. Once the water has reached a boil, add in the Brussels sprouts. Boil for 8 minutes or until soft.
5. Drain the Brussels sprouts into a colander.
6. Line a large baking sheet with parchment paper, or grease well using melted ghee.
7. Place the Brussels sprouts on the tray, allowing at least an inch of space between them for smashing.
8. Oil the bottom of a drinking glass and use it to smash each Brussels sprout so it is flat.
9. Brush the smashed sprouts with melted ghee and sprinkle with salt and pepper.
10. Bake at 400°F for about 30 minutes until the Brussels sprouts begin to turn brown and crispy.
11. While the Brussels sprouts bake, cook the bacon and grate the parmesan cheese.
12. Cut the bacon strips into ¼ inch pieces and cook over low heat, stirring frequently, until crispy.
13. After about 30 minutes of baking, remove the Brussels sprouts from the oven and flip each Brussels sprout. Top with grated cheese and return to the oven. Bake for an additional 10 minutes.
14. Remove from the oven. Sprinkle with bacon bits and serve.

Brussels sprouts might be the most controversial vegetable that there is—you either love them or you hate them. Give me a chance to make you love them! Add bacon, parmesan, and that extra crispness that can only be achieved by roasting, and I think there's a pretty good chance that you are going to find a new love for the humble Brussels sprout!

Roasted Delicata
with Cider Syrup

 4-6 servings

 50 minutes

½ gallon fresh apple cider
4 medium delicata squash
2 tablespoons ghee, melted
3 cloves garlic, minced
1 teaspoon salt

¼ teaspoon pepper
8–10 sprigs thyme, minced
4–5 sprigs rosemary, minced
¼ cup chèvre
¼ cup toasted pumpkin seeds

Directions

1. Begin by making the apple cider syrup. Place the apple cider in a medium saucepan and boil over high heat. Continue to boil until the cider has reduced to 1 cup. This takes over an hour, so it is best to do it ahead of time.
2. Next, prepare the squash. Preheat the oven to 400°F.
3. Cut the squash in half lengthwise and scoop out the seeds.
4. Slice into half circles, about ¼-inch in thickness.
5. Toss the squash rings together with the melted ghee, minced garlic, salt, pepper, thyme, and rosemary.
6. Spread the squash across two baking trays. Bake for 30–40 minutes.
7. To serve, drizzle warm cider syrup to taste and top with crumbled chèvre and toasted pumpkin seeds.

Fresh apple cider is such a unique ingredient, and it is only available for a couple of months out of the year. I always try to use it in as many creative ways as I can think of while the season lasts. The apple cider syrup in this recipe brings a unique flavor that enhances an already delicious roasted squash. And as an added bonus, when you boil the syrup down, it fills your home with a wonderful apple aroma!

Smashed Yukon Gem Potatoes

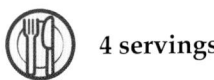 **4 servings**

 **1 hour 45 minutes**

2 pounds small to medium Yukon
Gem potatoes or other waxy potatoes
(about 12–16 potatoes)
3 tablespoons butter, melted
2–3 tablespoons salt, plus more to taste
Pepper, to taste
4 strips bacon

For the Sauce
3 tablespoons crispy chili brown
butter sauce (see p. 39)
1 cup sour cream

Directions

1. Preheat the oven to 400°F.
2. Scrub potatoes and place, with the skins still on, into a pot and cover with cold water.
3. Generously salt the water (2–3 tablespoons) and bring to a boil. Allow the potatoes to simmer for about 20–30 minutes or until soft when poked with a knife.
4. Drain the potatoes into a colander and allow them to steam for a few minutes.
5. Line two baking trays with parchment paper and drizzle with melted butter.
6. Place the potatoes on the parchment paper and smash flat using the bottom of a drinking glass.
7. Drizzle remaining butter over the smashed potatoes and sprinkle with salt and pepper.
8. Bake at 400°F for 1 hour or until the potatoes are crispy. You do not need to flip the potatoes.
9. While potatoes bake, cook bacon over low heat until crispy. Chop into small pieces.
10. To make the sauce, mix 3 tablespoons of melted Crispy Brown Butter Chili Sauce with 1 cup of sour cream.
11. To serve, sprinkle bacon on top of the smashed potatoes, and serve with the crispy chili sour cream on the side.

The creamy texture of Yukon Gem potatoes lends itself perfectly to this recipe — the insides of the potatoes are soft and creamy, complementing the crispy edges. Crispy Chili Brown Butter is one of my favorite flavors — I use it in several other recipes in this book — and it wonderfully complements this recipe when used in the sour cream topping.

Kale and Apple Salad

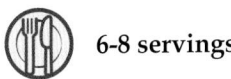 6-8 servings

 25 minutes

1 quart fresh apple cider
½ teaspoon salt, divided
⅛ teaspoon black pepper
2 medium beets
1 medium red onion

1 tablespoon ghee, melted
1 bunch kale (about a dozen leaves)
2 Pink Lady apples
½ cup pumpkin seeds, toasted

Directions

1. Begin by reducing the apple cider to make the dressing. Place the apple cider in a medium saucepan over medium-high heat. Boil the cider for about 20 minutes or until it has reduced down to ½ cup. Once the cider has reduced, stir in ¼ teaspoon salt and ⅛ teaspoon black pepper.
2. While the cider syrup reduces, prepare the rest of the ingredients.
3. Preheat the oven to 400°F.
4. Peel the beets and chop into roughly ¾-inch cubes.
5. Cut the onion into pieces of a similar size to the beets.
6. Toss with ¼ teaspoon salt and 1 tablespoon of ghee, spread on a baking sheet, and roast for 30 minutes.
7. Wash and roughly chop the kale.
8. Slice the apples into ⅛-inch slices.
9. In a large bowl, toss together all the ingredients with the dressing.

Sometimes simple is best, and this is certainly the case with this autumn kale salad. The sweetness of the roasted beets along with the tanginess of the apple cider reduction dressing is the perfect combination. Highlighting the flavors of fall, this recipe is my go-to for a potluck dish!

Pumpkin Pie Jars

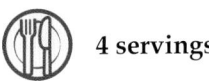 **4 servings**

 2 hours

For the Pumpkin Pie
1 cup pumpkin purée
½ cup maple syrup
1 cup cream
½ cup milk
⅛ teaspoon salt
4 egg yolks
2 whole eggs

For the Meringue
4 egg whites
¾ cup maple syrup

Directions

1. Start by preparing the pumpkin pie.
2. Preheat the oven to 325°F.
3. Place the pumpkin purée, maple syrup, cream, milk, and salt together in a small saucepan.
4. Heat over low heat until warm and stir to combine. Remove from heat.
5. Mix in the egg yolks and whole eggs and stir to combine. Make sure the mixture is smooth with no lumps.
6. Divide the mixture between 4 half-pint size mason jars. They will be full to the top with liquid.
7. Bake at 325°F for 45 minutes.
8. When the pumpkin pie jars are done baking, allow them to cool before making the meringue.
9. Place the egg whites in the bowl of a stand mixer fitted with the whisk attachment.
10. Place the maple syrup in a small saucepan over medium heat. Boil, stirring frequently, until the maple syrup reaches 240°F.
11. When the maple reaches about 235°F, begin whisking the egg whites on medium-high speed.

Continued on the next page...

12. When the egg whites are frothy and the maple syrup is at 240°F, begin slowly pouring the maple syrup into the egg whites, whisking on a high speed the whole time.
13. Once the maple syrup is fully incorporated, continue whisking on high speed for about 6 minutes or until stiff peaks form.
14. Spoon the meringue on top of the pie jars. Lightly caramelize with a blow torch until golden brown.
15. Serve the pumpkin pie jars soon after completing, the meringue is best when fresh.

Nothing is more classic than a pumpkin pie around Thanksgiving, but this mason jar dessert puts a little twist on the classic. The pie itself is not too sweet, with just a hint of maple bringing out the natural sweetness of the pumpkin. Topped with a soft, pillowy, torched meringue, this dessert will melt in your mouth.

Winter

Winter

Winter in Vermont is beautiful, but you have to learn to love it. Days are often overcast and gray, making the occasional sunny day even more sublime. The cold air bites at your cheeks and any exposed skin and catches in your throat when you first walk out the door, misty breath billowing up in a silver cloud. However, give yourself the chance and you will surely fall in love with the silent stillness of this season, and the contrast of the cold outside and the cozy living room woodstove.

Darkness falls as early as 4 o'clock, leaving no shortage of time to busy oneself in the kitchen. While the rush of spring, summer, and fall can sometimes keep us from devoting time to cooking, in winter there is no hurry, and the long, dark evenings offer the perfect chance to share food with the people you love.

The recipes in this chapter are warming, soothing, and cozy, highlighting the storage crops and animal products that carry us through the season.

Recipe Guide

Steak and Ale Pie

 6 servings

 3 hours 45 minutes

For the Filling
2 pound boneless chuck roast
1½ teaspoons salt, divided
2 medium onions
2 medium carrots
¼ cup chopped dried tomatoes
2–3 tablespoons ghee
2–3 cloves garlic, minced
1 teaspoon dried thyme
12 ounces pale ale

For the Mashed Potatoes
1½ pounds potatoes
½ cup cream
2 tablespoons butter
½ cup grated cheddar cheese
¾ teaspoon salt

Directions

1. Preheat the oven to 300°F.
2. Slice the chuck roast into 2-inch cubes. Season with 1 teaspoon of salt.
3. Prep the vegetables. Slice the onions, peel the carrots, and chop them into ½-inch cubes. Chop the dried tomatoes.
4. Preheat a Dutch oven over high heat. Melt ghee into the Dutch oven. Once the Dutch oven is hot, sear the beef in two batches to avoid overcrowding.
5. Once the beef has been seared, remove it from the Dutch oven, reduce heat to medium, add the onions, and sauté for one minute.
6. Add in the garlic, carrots, dried tomatoes, and dried thyme and sauté for another 1–2 minutes.
7. Return the beef to the pan and pour in the ale.
8. Bring the ale to a boil. Once it has reached a boil, remove from the heat, cover the Dutch oven with a lid, and place in the preheated oven.
9. Bake at 300°F for 2 hours.
10. After 2 hours, remove the pan from the oven and remove the lid. Increase the oven temperature to 375°F.

Continued on the next page...

11. Return the Dutch oven to the burner and boil over high heat for about 20–25 minutes until the liquid has reduced and thickened.
12. Shred the braised beef with two forks, and season with the remaining ½ teaspoon of salt or to taste.
13. For the mashed potato topping, peel the potatoes and cut them into quarters.
14. Place the potatoes in a large pot of salted water and bring to a boil.
15. Simmer the potatoes for about 15 minutes or until soft when poked with a fork.
16. Drain the potatoes into a colander.
17. In a small saucepan, heat the cream and butter until warm, but not boiling.
18. Mash the potatoes and pour in the cream and butter mixture, as well as the grated cheddar cheese and salt.
19. To assemble the finished dish, place the braised steak in the bottom of a 9-inch round pan. Spread the mashed potatoes over the top.
20. Place the dish back in the oven and bake at 375°F for 20–30 minutes until the mashed potatoes begin to brown.

This recipe combines two of my favorite English dishes—steak and ale pie, traditionally made in a shortcrust pastry, and shepherd's pie, traditionally made with a minced lamb layer topped with mashed potatoes. It's perfect for a rainy evening in the English countryside, where the inspiration comes from, or for a chilly Vermont night. Not only is it a great meal, it also leaves plenty of leftovers for the rest of the week.

Red Wine Braised Short Ribs

 4 servings

 3 hours 10 minutes

4 strips bacon
2 pounds bone-in short ribs
1 teaspoon salt
¼ teaspoon pepper
1 large onion
2 medium carrots

2–3 cloves garlic, minced
1 teaspoon dried thyme
1 teaspoon dried rosemary
2 cups beef stock
3 cups dry red wine

Directions

1. Preheat the oven to 325°F.
2. Chop bacon into ¼-inch pieces and place into a Dutch oven. Cook over low heat, stirring frequently until crispy.
3. Remove bacon from the Dutch oven and increase the heat to high.
4. Season the short ribs with salt and pepper and sear in the bacon grease for 3 minutes per side.
5. Remove the short ribs from the Dutch oven, pour off and discard excess fat.
6. Slice onions and peel and chop carrots.
7. Add the onions, carrots, garlic, dried thyme, and dried rosemary and sauté for 2–3 minutes.
8. Return the short ribs and bacon to the Dutch oven and pour in the beef stock and red wine. Bring to a boil. Once boiling, remove from heat and place a lid on the Dutch oven.
9. Place in the preheated oven and bake for 2½ hours.
10. After 2½ hours, remove from the oven and pour off the extra cooking liquid into a small saucepan. Place the saucepan over high heat and boil for 5–10 minutes or until the liquid has reduced to a sauce consistency and coats the back of a spoon.
11. Serve the short ribs over polenta or mashed potatoes, and top with the sauce.

The ultimate winter meal to warm you up. Red Wine Braised Short Ribs served over rich, creamy polenta will fill you up, nourish your body, and give you that burst of savory flavor that I always find myself craving in the winter months. This recipe is so simple to make, you can enjoy it on a weeknight, and yet with the proper presentation it makes a fantastic meal to share with guests.

Roasted Roots and Sausage

 6 servings

 1 hour 50 minutes

2 medium onions
4–5 cloves garlic, minced
¾ pound potatoes
¾ pound carrots
¾ pound sweet potatoes
¾ pound parsnips
¾ pound beets

1 pound Italian sausage
3–4 tablespoons ghee, melted
1½ teaspoon salt
¼ teaspoon black pepper
1 teaspoon dried thyme
1 teaspoon dried rosemary
1 tablespoon dried parsley

Directions

1. Preheat the oven to 400°F.
2. Peel and slice the onions and mince the garlic.
3. Peel potatoes, carrots, sweet potatoes, parsnips, and beets and cut into bite-sized pieces, approximately ½-inch by ½-inch.
4. Cut the sausage into bite-sized pieces.
5. Toss the veggies, and sausage with melted ghee, garlic, salt, pepper, and herbs.
6. Spread the mixture in a single layer across two baking sheets and bake at 400°F for 45–60 minutes, or until the root vegetables are soft and slightly brown.
7. Serve warm.

Roasted roots have always been a staple in my house. This recipe is easy to whip up and fills the need for a quick but nourishing meal during cold winter months. It always feels so nice to be able to rely on storage crops and have a meal that's entirely home-grown even in the thick of winter, and all of the root vegetables in this recipe are great for beginner gardeners.

Honey Glazed Chicken Legs

 6-8 servings

 55 minutes

2 tablespoons butter
1 tablespoon honey
3 cloves garlic, minced
⅛ teaspoon black pepper
¼ teaspoon dried chili
1 teaspoon dried thyme

1 teaspoon dried parsley
½ teaspoon dried winter savory
6 bone-in chicken thighs
6 chicken drumsticks
2 teaspoons salt

Directions

1. Preheat the oven to 400°F.
2. In a small saucepan combine the butter, honey, minced garlic, black pepper, dried chili, thyme, parsley, and winter savory.
3. Gently warm the mixture over a low heat until the butter is melted, and all the ingredients are combined. This gives the flavors a chance to infuse together.
4. Place the chicken on a baking sheet and generously salt both sides.
5. Spoon the glaze over the chicken thighs and drumsticks.
6. Bake at 400°F for 35 minutes or until the chicken reaches an internal temperature of 165°F.
7. Allow it to rest for 5 minutes before serving.

A little sweet, a little spicy, these glazed chicken legs hit the spot on a cold winter evening. The hint of chili provides a warming kick, and the sweet, sticky glaze is simply delicious every time. This is a family favorite and is an easy way to get dinner on the table quickly and easily. If you want a bigger meal, pair the chicken legs with roasted roots.

Stuffed Squash

 4-6 servings

 1 hour 45 minutes

3 small acorn squash
1½ teaspoons salt, divided
1 medium onion
1 large leek
2 stalks celery
2 Pink Lady apples
2 tablespoons ghee, divided

1 pound ground pork
2–3 cloves garlic, minced
1 teaspoon dried thyme
1 teaspoon dried sage
1 tablespoon maple syrup
¼ teaspoon black pepper
1 cup grated cheddar cheese

Directions

1. Preheat the oven to 400°F.
2. Cut the acorn squash in half, scoop out the seeds, and sprinkle with ½ teaspoon salt.
3. Place the squash cut side down on a baking sheet and bake for 45 minutes.
4. While the squash bakes, prepare the filling.
5. Dice the onion, cut the leek in half and slice into thin half circles, and slice the celery into small pieces. Peel and dice the apples.
6. Melt 1 tablespoon ghee in a cast iron skillet over high heat, when the pan is hot add the pork and cook, stirring occasionally until pork is cooked through.
7. Remove cooked pork from the pan and set aside.
8. Add in the onions, leek, celery and remaining ghee, and sauté for 2–3 minutes. Add the garlic and sauté for another minute. Add the diced apple and continue cooking for 1–2 minutes.
9. Remove from heat and add the cooked pork back to the pan along with thyme, sage, maple syrup, black pepper, and the remaining teaspoon of salt.
10. Once the squash is baked, remove from the oven. Fill each squash with the filling and top with grated cheddar cheese.
11. Return to the oven and bake for 10–15 minutes until the cheese is fully melted and begins to brown.

The apple and maple syrup in this recipe adds a nice bit of sweetness to what would otherwise be a savory dish. Apple and pork are a classic combo — throw in baked acorn squash and some spices and you really can't go wrong. This dish is a great weeknight dinner, and I like to pair it with the Apple Celeriac Salad (p. 175).

Kale and Sausage Soup

 6-8 servings

 45 minutes

1 pound Italian sausage
2 medium onions
1 pound potatoes
1 pound sweet potatoes
½ pound carrots
1 tablespoon ghee
2–3 cloves garlic, minced

1 tablespoon dried parsley
1 teaspoon dried thyme
1 teaspoon salt
¼ teaspoon black pepper
6 cups chicken broth
1 bunch kale, or 8 ounces frozen kale
3 cups cooked white beans

Directions

1. First, cut the sausages into ½-inch pieces and peel and slice the onions. Peel the potatoes, sweet potatoes, and carrots, and cut into bite-sized pieces, about ½-inch cubes.
2. Heat a large soup pot over medium heat. Melt ghee into the pot. Once warm, add the Italian sausage and sauté over medium heat for about 5 minutes. Add the onions and garlic and sauté for another 2 minutes.
3. Add the potatoes, sweet potatoes, carrots, dried herbs, salt, and pepper and sauté for another minute.
4. Add the chicken broth and bring to a boil. Allow to simmer for about 20 minutes until the potatoes, sweet potatoes, and carrots are soft.
5. While the soup simmers, prepare the kale by chopping it into bite-sized pieces.
6. Add the kale and cooked white beans and remove from heat, allowing the residual heat to lightly cook the kale.
7. Adjust the seasoning to taste and serve.

This soup is a great hearty winter soup. You can use frozen kale in this recipe, or if you're lucky to have a local farm growing kale in a greenhouse, fresh kale is great too! Sweet potatoes add a pop of color and sweetness, the sausage adds some savory and spicy flavor, and the beans make the soup hearty and comforting—perfect for a cold day!

Beer Cheddar Soup

 2 servings   **1 hour**

1 large onion
2 stalks celery
2 medium potatoes
1–2 tablespoons butter
2–3 cloves garlic, minced
1 12-ounce can IPA

2 cups chicken stock
2 cups grated extra sharp cheddar cheese
⅛ teaspoon crushed dried chili
½ teaspoon dried thyme
⅓ cup cream
½ teaspoon salt

Directions

1. Prepare the vegetables: slice the onion, chop the celery into small pieces, and peel and chop the potatoes into ½-inch cubes.
2. In a medium saucepan, melt the butter over medium heat.
3. Sauté the onions and garlic for 1–2 minutes. Add the chopped celery and sauté for another 1–2 minutes.
4. Add the IPA and boil for 3–5 minutes until it is reduced by half.
5. Add the potatoes and the chicken stock and bring to a boil.
6. Reduce the heat and allow the soup to simmer for 15–20 minutes or until the potatoes are soft.
7. Remove the soup from the heat and immediately melt in the cheese and add the dried chili and dried thyme.
8. Using an immersion blender, blend the soup until smooth.
9. Stir in the cream and season with salt to taste.
10. Serve.

You can't really get more Vermont than sharp cheddar cheese. Or maybe you can—add a locally brewed IPA to your soup and you're looking at two of Vermont's most iconic ingredients. You can use your favorite IPA, and since the soup only requires 12 ounces, there should be plenty left to crack open to enjoy alongside your soup.

Vermont-Style Baked Beans

 6-8 servings

 5 hours

2 cups Marfax dry beans
4 slices bacon
1 medium onion, diced
2–3 cloves garlic, minced
¼ cup canned tomato sauce

½ cup maple syrup
1 tablespoon apple cider vinegar
1 teaspoon salt
¼ teaspoon black pepper

Directions

1. For best results, soak the beans in 1 quart of water and 2¼ teaspoons of salt overnight. Once done soaking, rinse the beans thoroughly to remove the salt.
2. Cover the rinsed beans in water and bring to a boil. Simmer the beans for 30 minutes to partially cook them.
3. Preheat the oven to 325°F.
4. Drain the beans but save 1 cup of the cooking liquid.
5. Slice the bacon into ½-inch pieces and cook over low heat in a Dutch oven until crispy.
6. Add onions and garlic and sauté for another 1–2 minutes.
7. Add tomato sauce, maple syrup, apple cider vinegar, partially cooked beans, and the 1 cup of cooking liquid. Bring the mixture to a boil. Once boiling, remove from the heat and cover with a lid.
8. Place the pot in the preheated oven and bake for about 3–4 hours, checking every hour and adding more water as necessary. The beans are done when they are soft and creamy.
9. When the beans have finished cooking, add in salt and pepper and serve.

These baked beans take several hours to cook, and while they cook, they fill your whole house with a wonderfully sweet maple aroma, leaving you anticipating the sweet and savory delicious dinner that is coming. I like to use Marfax beans for this recipe. This heirloom variety is easy to grow and offers the best creamy texture of any bean, but really any kind of dry bean will work wonderfully.

Cheesy Parsnip Apple Bake

 6 servings

 2 hours

2 large onions
2 tablespoons of butter
1½ teaspoons salt, divided
2 pounds parsnips
3 Pink Lady apples

2 cups grated cheddar cheese
1 cup cream
1 cup whole milk
2–3 cloves garlic, minced
½ teaspoon dried thyme

Directions

1. Preheat the oven to 400°F.
2. Begin by caramelizing the onions. Slice the onions and melt 2 tablespoons of butter into a large skillet over low heat.
3. Add sliced onions to the skillet along with ½ teaspoon of salt and cook, stirring occasionally until the onions are caramelized.
4. While the onions caramelize, prep the other ingredients.
5. Peel the parsnips and apples and thinly slice.
6. In a small saucepan, combine the cream, milk, minced garlic, thyme, and the remaining 1 teaspoon of salt, and gently warm until hot but not boiling.
7. Remove from the heat and begin assembling the dish.
8. In a 9x11-inch pan, begin layering parsnips, apples, caramelized onions, grated cheese, and cream mixture. Repeat these layers until the pan is full and the ingredients are used up. Top with grated cheese.
9. Bake at 400°F for 1 hour and 10 minutes or until soft when poked with a fork and browned on top.
10. Remove from the oven, allow to cool slightly before serving.

Delicious creamy layers of baked parsnip, apple, and cheddar cheese perfectly complement one another in this sweet and salty casserole. Using apples and parsnips that have been stored in the root cellar since the fall harvest, this dish is a great example of utilizing storage crops throughout the winter and gives you the gift of these fall flavors long into the cold winter days.

Cabbage Steak with Hot Honey Glaze

 4 servings

 55 minutes

1 medium cabbage
2 tablespoons ghee, melted
½ teaspoon salt
4 tablespoons honey

1 teaspoon dried chili
4 cloves garlic, minced
1 teaspoon cider vinegar
½ teaspoon black pepper

Directions

1. Preheat the oven to 425°F.
2. Slice the cabbage into four circles, roughly ¾ of an inch thick.
3. Place cabbage slices on a baking sheet, brush both sides with melted ghee, and sprinkle with salt.
4. Roast at 425°F for 40 minutes until browned and crispy around the edges.
5. While the cabbage bakes, prepare the glaze.
6. In a small saucepan, combine the honey, chili, minced garlic, apple cider vinegar, and black pepper and warm gently over low heat until it begins to bubble. Remove from heat and allow flavors to infuse while the cabbage continues to bake in the oven.
7. After 40 minutes, remove the cabbage from the oven, spoon the glaze over the cabbage steaks, and serve warm.

Cabbage is one of my favorite vegetables. So versatile and an excellent storage crop, easy to grow for beginner gardeners, and there is so much creativity in how to cook and prepare it. I think cabbage is often overlooked and disregarded, but these cabbage steaks will be sure to change some people's opinion of the vegetable itself. Simple to prepare, the hot honey glaze brings out the flavor of the cabbage and adds some of its own.

Fondant Potatoes

 4 servings

 45 minutes

6 large waxy potatoes
½ tablespoon ghee
3 tablespoons butter
4 cloves garlic, bashed
½ teaspoon salt

¼ teaspoon black pepper
1 teaspoon dried thyme
1 teaspoon dried rosemary
1 cup chicken stock

Directions

1. Preheat the oven to 400°F.
2. Peel the potatoes and cut the top and bottom ends off so the potatoes can stand up on their own.
3. In a large cast iron skillet, heat ½ tablespoon of ghee over medium to high heat.
4. Sear the potatoes for 4–6 minutes on each side until golden brown.
5. Lower the heat to low, add the butter, bashed garlic cloves, salt, black pepper, thyme, and rosemary.
6. Baste the potatoes for 1–2 minutes, spooning the butter over the tops of the potatoes repeatedly.
7. Add the chicken stock.
8. Place the skillet in the oven and bake uncovered for 35 minutes, or until the potatoes are soft all the way though and most of the stock has evaporated.
9. Serve warm.

Fondant potatoes are sure to impress at any dinner party or family gathering. These golden brown potatoes are paired with the flavors of garlic, thyme, and rosemary and cooked until the centers are creamy and delicious. Using only potatoes and other pantry staples, the ingredients for this dish can easily be sourced locally all winter long, and you can make this dish on a whim as you most likely have all of the ingredients on hand.

Apple Celeriac Salad

 6-8 servings

 20 minutes

For the Dressing
⅓ cup apple cider vinegar
¼ cup olive oil
¼ cup maple syrup
½ teaspoon salt
¼ teaspoon black pepper

For the Salad
1 medium celeriac
3 medium carrots
3 Pink Lady apples
¼ cup cooked bacon bits
½ cup toasted pumpkin seeds

Directions

1. First, prepare the dressing by whisking together the cider vinegar, olive oil, maple syrup, salt, and black pepper.
2. Next, prepare the vegetables for the salad.
3. Peel the celeriac and carrots and shred and then place in a large bowl.
4. Thinly slice the apples, leaving the skins on, and add to the bowl.
5. Immediately, to prevent the apples from browning, toss the shredded celeriac and carrots, sliced apples, bacon bits, and pumpkin seeds together with the dressing.
6. Serve.

It can be hard to find a fresh, seasonal salad recipe in the middle of winter, but this one is a winner! The crunch of the celeriac and carrots makes this salad refreshing and delicious, and it is easy to make a big batch to share with guests or enjoy as leftovers. If you're going to make this salad ahead, simply wait to add the pumpkin seeds and bacon until just before serving so they maintain their crunch! This salad makes a great side when served with our Stuffed Squash (p. 161).

Roasted Beet Salad

 6-8 servings

 1 hour 20 minutes

2½ pounds beets
2 tablespoon butter, divided
1 teaspoon salt, divided
⅛ teaspoon black pepper
2 medium onions

2 tablespoons apple cider vinegar
1 tablespoon maple syrup
¼ cup toasted pumpkin seeds
2 ounces chèvre

Directions

1. Preheat the oven to 400°F.
2. Peel and chop the beets into eighths.
3. Place the beets on a baking tray. Melt 1 tablespoon of butter and toss the beets with the melted butter, ½ teaspoon of salt and black pepper.
4. Roast at 400°F for about 1 hour, until beets are soft when poked with a fork.
5. While the beets roast, cook the onions. Heat a cast iron skillet over medium heat, add the remaining 1 tablespoon of butter.
6. Slice the onions. Once the butter has melted in the pan, add in the onions and the remaining ½ teaspoon of salt.
7. Cook the onions, stirring occasionally until they are caramelized.
8. When the beets are cooked, remove from the oven, mix with caramelized onions, apple cider vinegar, maple syrup, toasted pumpkin seeds, and crumbled chèvre.

Eating the rainbow can be hard to achieve in the depths of winter, that's why this roasted beet salad always brings that needed pop of color to the table. Beautifully roasted beets from storage combined with caramelized onions and crumbled goat cheese makes for a nice warm winter salad and this dish is a great addition to any meal.

Red Wine Poached Pears

 6 servings

 45 minutes

For Pears
6 pears
3 cups dry red wine
¾ cup maple syrup
3 cups water

For the Maple Cream
1 cup mascarpone cheese
2 tablespoons maple syrup

Directions

1. Peel the pears and remove the core and seeds from the middle using an apple corer, hollowing out the center of the pear.
2. In a medium saucepan, combine the red wine, maple syrup, and water.
3. Bring the liquid to a boil and add the pears, making sure they are fully submerged. If they are not fully submerged, turn them regularly as they simmer.
4. Reduce the heat and allow the pears to simmer for 20–25 minutes or until soft. The cooking time will vary slightly depending on the ripeness of the pears.
5. Once cooked, remove the pears from the liquid. Place the pot with the poaching liquid over high heat and boil vigorously for about 15–25 minutes until it has reduced down to a thick syrup.
6. For the maple cream, combine the mascarpone and maple syrup and whisk together.
7. Serve the poached pears with the maple cream and a drizzle of red wine syrup.

The rich burgundy color of these pears is wonderfully attention grabbing in the depths of winter when colorful foods are hard to find. This recipe is simple, but so elegant that it is certain to impress guests. It is one of those low effort, big reward recipes! Pears store nicely in a root cellar for several months, so this recipe is best enjoyed in the first half of winter.

Maple Fudge

 **6 servings**    **30 minutes**

2 cups maple syrup
1 cup cream
3 tablespoons unsalted butter

Directions

1. Line a 9x5-inch pan with parchment paper and set aside.
2. Place the maple syrup in a small saucepan over medium heat and bring to a boil. Once boiling add the cream.
3. Continue to boil, stirring occasionally until the mixture reaches 236°F. This will take about 20 minutes.
4. Cut the chilled butter into ½-inch cubes.
5. Once the mixture reaches 236°F, remove from heat and add in the butter.
6. Whisk the butter in.
7. Continue whisking vigorously as the mixture cools for about 6½ minutes until the fudge begins to thicken.
8. After the fudge thickens, pour it into the prepared pan. Allow to cool completely before cutting.

With only three ingredients, this maple fudge is so easy to make and is guaranteed to bring back nostalgic childhood memories of eating fudge at grandma's house—that is, if your childhood was anything like mine. Make this recipe to serve as a dessert or simply to give as gifts to the most important people in your life.

Substitutions Guide

As I trained to become a chef and grew more and more comfortable with understanding cooking techniques and ingredients, I began to trust my intuition. Suddenly, cooking became something creative that allowed me to connect the land around me to my style of cooking, and the food I liked to eat began to ebb and flow with the seasons and where I was in the world. This isn't to say that everyone who reads this book must be a master chef, completely un-reliant on recipes, but we do hope that this book encourages you to cook intuitively. Our hope is for these recipes to act as a guide and a source of inspiration, rather than as a rigid list of instructions that must be followed to a tee. Understanding how to make intuitive substitutions based on what products you have access to is the first step to becoming an intuitive cook.

The intention of this guide is to provide a reference point when making common substitutions that could come up through a number of recipes in this book, in the hopes of empowering you to use ingredients that are available to you locally depending on your location and time of year.

— Nora

Cooking Oils

The primary cooking oil used in this book is ghee. Ghee is clarified butter, meaning the purified fat from butter. Ghee has a higher smoke point than butter, making it a great option for high heat cooking. Ghee is used in this book for searing meat or vegetables at a high temperature or for roasting vegetables at a high temperature, where regular butter would burn. We chose ghee because it is a dairy product and is one of the few cooking fats that can be easily sourced from Vermont or made at home by melting butter and removing the milk solids. Alternative cooking fats with a high enough smoke point for searing and roasting at high temperatures include animal fats such as lard, beef tallow, or duck fat. If cooking for vegetarians or if you simply do not have access to any of these fats, canola oil, vegetable oil, or avocado oil are all excellent options. Of course, these fats cannot be sourced locally from Vermont, but from a culinary standpoint are all excellent options if ghee is not something that you have in your pantry.

Greens

Many recipes in this book call for a specific leafy green vegetable, for example, kale in the Kale and Sausage Soup, or spinach in the Spring Omelet. Most leafy green vegetables behave similarly when cooked and add similar flavors and textures, so there is a fair amount of freedom to substitute one leafy green vegetable for another depending on what you have abundant in your garden or at the local farmers' market. When green vegetables are called for, keep in mind the option to substitute for any of the following: spinach, kale, arugula, Swiss chard, collard greens, mustard greens, or beet greens.

Stock or Broth

Many recipes call for chicken stock in this book, but it's important to remember that the type of stock or broth can be changed and the recipe will turn out just fine. If you are cooking for vegetarians, feel free to use vegetable stock instead, or if you are looking for a richer flavor profile, perhaps try beef stock!

Root Vegetables

Many recipes call for storage crops and root vegetables such as parsnips, potatoes, carrots, sweet potatoes, and celeriac. These starchy storage crops will all have similar cook times when roasted, so feel free to make substitutes based on what you have in storage or add in similar root veggies such as rutabaga and turnips.

Herbs

This book uses a mix of fresh and dried herbs depending on the season. Fresh herbs tend to have more flavor and are always preferable if they are available. Some herbs like rosemary are easy to grow indoors and can add a flavor punch all winter long, but others are easier to harvest when they are abundant in the summer months and can be dried to be used in the winter. Always use fresh herbs if they are available, but if not, you can substitute for an equal quantity of dried herbs.

Final Thoughts

The idea for this book was born a few years ago. I had just moved back to Vermont, the place where Jenna and I had grown up and where Jenna had remained, working to transform her small piece of land into a bountiful homestead. All the ingredients were in place: two Vermont sisters, a little bit too much free time, and a burning question.

"Is it possible to make a cookbook using only Vermont grown ingredients?"

We had seen a number of other farm to table cookbooks set in Vermont, highlighting locally grown ingredients…but we wanted to take it one step further. We wanted to create a book using only Vermont grown ingredients, ones that would be readily available and easy to find.

With this goal in mind, we decided to exclude ingredients that could technically be grown in Vermont but that would be difficult to find. That meant that things like wheat and rice were off the table because while they certainly can be grown in Vermont, they aren't accessible, easy to find or convenient to grow on a small scale.

At first it felt a little unnatural. As a chef, I had become used to certain strategies: reaching for a little lemon juice to brighten flavors here and there, or adding a pinch of sugar to bring a little sweetness, or a dash of vanilla extract to make a dessert pop. With these ingredients out of bounds, I began to ask myself new questions and get a little more creative.

"What could replace lemon juice that is grown in Vermont?" "Would using maple syrup instead of sugar work in this dish?" These were the questions I would mutter to myself, scrawling thoughts down on a scrap of paper in the kitchen, while some new experimental sauce boiled away on the stove behind me. This process forced me to evaluate and think more creatively about each recipe than I had ever had to do in the past.

At first, I was annoyed whenever I couldn't use a standard ingredient, something that I would normally have put into a recipe without a second thought. But as time went on and I got used to relying on Vermont staples, the recipe development began to feel easier. In fact, the recipes almost began to write themselves: as it turns out, flavors that go well together are often the things that are in season at the same time. After all, that is what makes a cohesive cuisine. Italian food is good because it leans on ingredients that are abundant in a certain region of the world at a certain time of year. That those ingredients just happen to complement each other is one of the many wonders of the world!

In the end, and with the exception of salt, pepper, and oil, we succeeded in creating 60 recipes using only local ingredients that are readily available. Writing this book helped me understand "Vermont cuisine" in a way I hadn't previously, and through this process I have developed a deeper understanding of how to weave together the flavors from the part of the world that I am lucky enough to call home. We hope that this book has helped to do the same for you. Whether you also call Vermont your home or are a visitor to our unique and beautiful state we hope that this book has provided you with a greater appreciation for Vermont and all that it has to offer.

— Nora

As a home gardener and homesteader, for years I have been fascinated with farm to table food and obsessed with the idea of creating meals exclusively from homegrown and local ingredients. In our early homesteading days, my husband and I would often get very excited when we managed to put together an "all homegrown meal."

Working with Nora to create this cookbook has truly broadened my horizon when it comes to cooking with local ingredients. Putting an all homegrown meal on the table feels easily within reach when I reference this cookbook, and I hope that the same will be true for our readers. I can say with complete honesty that I frequently reference the recipes in this book for my own home cooking.

It was a great joy to be able to work with my sister and bring together my passion as a photographer and my hobbies of farming and gardening to create a cookbook that will hopefully help many like-minded people create delicious meals.

— Jenna

Index

Scan the QR code
to visit our website:
vermontfarmtotable.net

01 14